EVERYDAY
MIRACLES

A STORY OF SURVIVAL MIRACLES AND BLESSINGS

JUDIE DIETZLER

Copyright © 2019 by Judie Dietzler.

ISBN   Softcover   978-1-950580-40-8
        Ebook   978-1-950580-48-4

All rights reserved. No part of this book may be reproduced or transmitted in any form or by any means, electronic or mechanical, including photocopying, recording, or by any information storage and retrieval system without express written permission from the author, except in the case of brief quotations embodied in critical reviews and certain other non-commercial uses permitted by copyright law.

Printed in the United States of America.

To order additional copies of this book, contact:
Bookwhip
1-855-339-3589
https://www.bookwhip.com

I didn't believe I had experienced or witnessed any miracles but after May 16, 2016 I witnessed a very powerful miracle and when I began writing my manuscript, I realized there had been so many miracles throughout my life. That fateful date in May I almost lost the most important person in my life but once again I experienced one of God's miracles and he watched over my husband and protected him from a near fatal car accident.

As I began to write the story of my life, many painful memories included, I not only realized that God had protected Ron but, he had been walking beside me all of my life.

Because there had been so much abuse and neglect throughout my life, I had blocked out the memories of most of my childhood and early teen years. I believe when a traumatized mind is ready to remember, it will release the memories. I only remembered bits and pieces of my past but, as I started to write the book, suddenly memories from my past started to flow on the pages of the computer, and tears started to flow as well.

I initially decided to tell my story because I felt it would be healing for me to release the emotions from the past. The trauma and miracles I experienced so many years ago could also be important for someone else so they will realize they are not alone.

But the number one reason for writing my story in the first place was to learn from the past, make peace with it and close it so I could finally enjoy the peace I have obtained in the present and look to the future with no regrets.

I was in church recently and an inner voice said "This book isn't about me. ***The story is about how God has walked beside me throughout my life,***" so I need to change the book so readers will understand that he is always with us even in the most difficult times. Some of the things that happened were devastating and no one should go through my ordeal but, when you read the entire story you will see it is possible to survive and thrive with God and a caring church family.

I would like to share several experiences that have happened during my life, many of which were so traumatic that I blocked them from my memory until I started on the journey of writing my story. But as I started to remember each event another revelation came to pass, ***I was not alone on my journey.*** There was only one thing that could have brought me through some of the events that happened in my childhood and adult years and that was the presence of God and his guidance.

I went to church when I was young but I was not raised in a Christian home, however, I did manage to turn to God when I was desperate. What was surprising to me was that he was also protecting me even when I was not on my knees asking for his help.

He must have seen goodness in me that I couldn't see in myself.

Have you ever felt unworthy of anyone's love, including Gods? You just didn't think you could measure up. That's the way I felt most of my life. I always had to prove myself and show that I was pretty or could make the grade, etc. I was used by my step-dad and my grandpa and somewhere along the way I decided to hurt before I got hurt so I put a protective shell around my heart and wouldn't let anyone get too close.

But God loves you no matter what and through the years he has always been beside me and finally thirty years ago he sent me an angel in human form to take care of me, and protect me.

He saw through that extroverted exterior and saw a vulnerable person that had been hurt and needed protection and, that is what he vowed to do, and that is what he has done for all these years until a fateful day in May of 2016 when both of our worlds came crashing down, but we did have someone looking after us that day: God.

I am going to start with the 2016 ***"Miracle"*** when I almost lost the most important person in my life and, it brought me to my knees making me realize that throughout my life I had been experiencing ***"God's Miracles,"*** not realizing that it had been his footsteps walking beside me, when I thought I was alone.

From there I will backtrack through other painful areas of my life, many were buried deep in my subconscious, never wanting to surface, until I began writing on the pages of this book.

Throughout the pages I share the *lessons I have learned* from fifty years of experience, and how I know today that "God" and his "Miracles" were at work in my life even during the darkest, most painful times in my life. I will show you at what point an **"Everyday Miracle"** was present. Pay close attention! Miracles don't just happen in my life. Pray, talk to God, and pay attention. Miracles can also happen in your life.

I hope my experience may help you know that you are not alone, even if you don't have a family or friends you need to remember **YOU ARE NOT ALONE.** Someone is walking beside you.

CONTENTS

Chapter 1.	A Legacy Nearly Dies Through Tragedy	1
Chapter 2.	Painful Past/Shattered Legacy	21
Chapter 3.	Did You Ask The Right Questions to Change the Outcome of Your Legacy?	45
Chapter 4.	Legacy of Love	73
Chapter 5.	Family Legacy	92
Chapter 6.	Legacy Careers	106
Chapter 7.	Legacy of Healing	124
Chapter 8.	Legacy of Friendship	144
Chapter 9.	Legacy of Service	163
Chapter 10.	Legacy Life Lessons	171
Chapter 11.	Legacy of a Parent	184
Chapter 12.	Celebrities from the Past	188
Chapter 13.	Life's Craziest Moment	190
Chapter 14.	Legacy of a Hero	207
Chapter 15.	Legacy Milestones	216
Chapter 16.	Leave A Worthy Legacy	224
Chapter 17.	Legacy Life Lessons	229
Chapter 18.	Will Your Legacy "Dash" Live On?	234
Chapter 19.	The Miracle of "Everyday Miracles"	238

CHAPTER 1

A LEGACY NEARLY DIES THROUGH TRAGEDY

Never Say Never Miracles Happen Every Day

On May 14, 2016 81-year-old Ron left for a car show in Payette, Idaho in his award winning white 1959 Ford Thunderbird that I bought him for Christmas thirty years ago but he never made it to his destination. Right before the Payette, Idaho off-ramp he was struck by a 2007 Hummer going at an excessive speed after the driver drank, stayed up all night, and fell asleep at the wheel.

The Thunderbird rolled several times, landing on its top with my husband pinned in the car and gas leaking out. The roof of the car was flat on the door panels with Ron wedged underneath. The fire department emergency team had to use crow bars to pull open the door in order to extract him from the vehicle. He was immediately rushed to the closest hospital for stabilization.

I received a call from a highway patrol officer stating that my husband had been in a *slight* automobile accident and he was in the West Valley Medical Center in Caldwell, Idaho. The first thing I did was call one of my friends and her husband because I was so scared and I needed someone that I felt we could count on.

I picked them because Paul and Ron were baseball buddies. They would email back and forth about how the Chicago Cubs were playing during the baseball season. Ron didn't have very many close friends and when he opened his eyes, I wanted him to be surrounded by friendly faces. The first people that most people call would be their family but in our case our sons always put us on the back burner. My impression is that we are an afterthought.

I knew that Ron was going to need people around him that loved him 100% of the time and would drop everything to take care of him and were willing to put the rest of their life and activities on hold if necessary.

I had asked both sons to stop by on rare occasions to help with different things that required getting on a ladder and they were always too busy so I couldn't take a chance with something this important. Ron had taken care of me for thirty years and I wasn't going to let him down when he needed me, even if it meant stepping on toes.

I jumped in the car and raced over to Caldwell but as soon as I got there, I knew it wasn't a minor accident. He was there only long enough for them to stabilize his condition and then they transported him to St Alphonsus Hospital in Boise, Idaho because they had the only trauma unit.

Paul and Kathy arrived almost at the same time. Ron looked so small and helpless in his hospital bed. The Sheriff took pictures of him for their report and they told me they transported the other driver to the Fruitland, Idaho emergency room but he had been walking around and the paramedics had checked him at the scene of the accident.

I will never understand why they did not do a breathalyzer test at the scene of the accident but waited until hours later to do a blood test at the hospital.

Ron was admitted to the Boise, Idaho hospital and once again his vitals had to be stabilized. He had three broken bones in his neck, a crushed vertebra in his lower back, and his left arm was completely broken in half which would require surgery. (He is left handed). He couldn't have surgery for two days because he was on Xarelto (a blood thinner) due to blood clots he had two years earlier.

The paramedics that arrived on the accident scene said they didn't expect the Thunderbird driver had survived the accident because the car had flipped three or four times, landed on its top and totally flattened, pinning Ron inside with gas leaking. He regained consciousness briefly and asked "How's my car and how's the other driver?"

They asked if anyone else was in the car with him and he said "Yes" They asked "Who?" He said "God!" **Miracles can happen even when you have great loss and tragedy.**

Ron misses having his beautiful one of a kind 1959 Thunderbird every day and hasn't been able to find a replacement for his trophy car.

He was in the trauma center for ten days and from there he was transferred to a rehabilitation center for another fourteen days. It took a lot to help him recover. He doesn't remember the accident from the time he was hit because he blacked out and was unconscious, only remembering bits and pieces.

We have a little Shih Tzu Dog that was five years old at the time. I think he must have Velcro attaching his body to my husband's leg because everywhere my husband goes, PePeLePew goes. From the time Ron went in the hospital Pepe didn't sleep at night. He paced the floor, whining and crying like a baby. I would put him in bed with me and tell him that Daddy would be home soon but that didn't help. He only stayed in the bed for about fifteen minutes, got down on the floor and started pacing once more.

Pepe wasn't getting any sleep and neither was I so there was only one solution to the problem, conceal and sneak him into the hospital and Ron's rehabilitation center. Pepe needed to see his Daddy. Once he saw Ron, he was OK, at least for twenty-four hours. Once he made it to the rehabilitation center, they would let me bring him home for short visits and he would sit on the front porch with Pepe on his lap.

Once he was home Ron's long recovery included:

- Helping him heal from his injuries with his daily and weekly therapy sessions.

- Ron had to deal with the pain & sadness of no longer having a Classic Thunderbird.

- He had the disappointment of no longer being a member of the Thunderbird Club that he started.

- How to work with an attorney that goes after his client's insurance company instead of the driver who caused the accident & his insurance company.

The severity of the wreck has made a huge impact on the health of my husband, and we have not got so much as an "I'm Sorry for such a thoughtless act." It was a miracle that he survived the wreck but he did promise to take care of me forever and he isn't one to break a promise.

Oscar was a nineteen-year-old kid from New Plymouth, Idaho but he borrowed the 2007 black Hummer from his grandfather so he could drive forty-five miles to party with his friends. His grandpa didn't drive or have a driver's license but he owned eight vehicles and, in my opinion, he had minimal insurance on all eight vehicles.

Why did he own so many vehicles? Grandpa is from Mexico and does not speak English and it appears that the majority of his friends are also from Mexico, also don't speak English and don't appear to have credit. Grandpa may either be making money selling the vehicles or he is buying the cars & letting other people that are not US residents use them out of the goodness of his heart. I feel he is probable selling both the vehicles and the insurance to the people that are unable to get credit.

At one time I was insurance licensed and if I remember correctly that could be a liability problem for the person that might have an accident with anyone that has purchased one of the vehicles from Oscar's grandpa. If you are in an accident with one of grandpa's vehicles but you are not an authorized driver or authorized on the insurance policy there could be a problem. I am not sure how you can be authorized on either if you are not related to grandpa and your name is not on the title of the car as the owner, but at the time all I wanted to do was put my husband back together.

I feel that whatever they are doing could be serious problem and eventually other people besides my husband may get hurt, killed or in prison. I feel sorry for the people that live in the Payette, Idaho and surrounding area that could possibly get in a car accident with one of the vehicles that has been sold by Oscar's grandpa.

There may not be a problem with grandpa buying vehicles and loaning them or selling them to help other people that are not as fortunate if he is doing it for the right reason. But is the person who is buying the vehicle an authorized driver on the policy? If he is selling the vehicle, including the insurance but the title remains in grandpa's name until the car is paid for then there may be a problem if the driver has an auto accident before they are considered the owner of the vehicle.

My personal thought is grandpa doesn't have basic knowledge of auto insurance or he would have had more than $25,000 in insurance because it isn't enough insurance to cover a major auto accident.

He shouldn't have let his nineteen-year-old grandson drive his HUMMER unless he knew he had common sense and grandpa needed strict ground rules for the driving of the vehicle. He should have had a curfew for the return of the Hummer, (which should have been by 11:00 pm the night before the accident occurred.)

If grandpa or parents had set the appropriate guidelines for Oscar, he would not have been out drinking all night and on the road in the wee hours of May 14, 2016 with what ended up as a dangerous killing machine. So, they can take more than their share of responsibility for the near death on May 14, 2016 and the fact that an eighty-one-year-old man had his prized possession destroyed next to the Fruitland/Payette exit. The judge should have ordered you to replace his dream. That would have helped ease the pain of the loss you left in the middle of the highway.

Oscar first headed for the Cherry Blossom Festival in Emmett, Idaho with his girlfriend and at some point, he ended up in Boise, Idaho in the wee hours of May 14, 2016. At approximately 6:00 am he decided to stop and get something to eat on his way back to Payette where his grandpa lived. Around 7:00 am he got back in his car headed for Payette. He started getting drowsy from being up all night, drinking and eating so he pulled over for a couple of minutes but a few minutes later instead of sleeping it off he started once again down the highway, full speed ahead. He kept dozing so he rolled down all of the windows but instead of heeding the warning signs to pull over he continued, after all he was nearing an exit and *closing in on what could be the final resting place for an eighty-one-year-old man and his beloved show car.*

Who do you think Oscar's parents were thinking about in their household when Oscar called them and told them about the automobile accident? The eighty-one-year-old man that was fighting for his life in a trauma center? Or keeping the nineteen-year-old that had been drinking, speeding and driving along with grandpa from spending time in jail, prison, or paying restitution to the eighty-one-year-old man?

Out of the three residents only one had been a US citizen all of his life and had obeyed all of the US laws that entire time. He also has had a US driver's license for sixty-five years and has paid United States taxes the seventy years he worked.

How did things turn out? Grandpa's minimal Progressive insurance policy had a $25,000 policy coverage. Out of the $25,000 that was paid out, Medicare received an $11,000.00 reimbursement, our attorney received $7,000, and my husband, who almost died, received $6,000. In addition, his award winning one of a kind 1959 thunderbird was destroyed by a kid without a single brain cell in his head. If he had a brain he wouldn't have been driving after a night of drinking.

For his part in turning my husband's dream into a nightmare, Oscar got off with a slap on the wrist. His grandpa's insurance company had to pay $25,000 which was a drop in the bucket for the damage their client's grandson caused. Oscar was required to take a few "Logical Thinking" classes and he had to pay a restitution to Ron of $1200.00 which he has been paying $48.00 per month.

What happened to Grandpa? Nothing as far as I can tell. He's probably still buying and selling vehicles to other non-residents that don't have credit and the Payette motor vehicle department and insurance department don't seem to think what he is doing is a problem.

Maybe it will be a problem if the next person dies. Maybe the Payette court will pay attention if grandpa is the one that is in the hot seat and he has to tell the judge face to face that he doesn't have a driver's license, he doesn't drive but he tells the judge that he needs all of the vehicles. Grandpa never saw the inside of the courtroom. It was his decisions that started the chain of events but he was able to walk away without being held accountable.

Let's see if any reputable insurance company will give him auto insurance on all of his vehicles if he is in prison. We had to sign a form with the Progressive Insurance company that we wouldn't sue them or their client or they wouldn't pay the $25,000 that we only received $6,000 of the $25,000.

Ron only had four loves in this world: God, me, Pepe (our Shih Tzu dog) and his beloved 1959 Thunderbird in that order. I gave him the Thunderbird for Christmas thirty years ago and he pampered that car. The very next year he started the Vintage 1958-1969 Thunderbird Club. He was the President of the club for the first ten years.

Our garage walls are covered with trophies and plaques from the many car shows that his beautiful car won. There were only four- hundred 1959 thunderbirds left in the world, minus one now, which leaves 399. Ron had the engine rebuilt in 2008 along with having several engine parts chromed.

But Miracles do happen and sometimes God intervenes and I believe that is what happened a month before the car accident. In March of 2016 Ron registered for the Boise Roadster Show. Scott Newell called and said he was planning on having a special display with four vehicles and he wanted Ron's car to be one of the four because the Thunderbird had won first place in last year's Roadster show. Scott purchased special jackets and hats for the four participants since they were not eligible for trophies. As far as Ron was concerned, he was far more impressed with the jacket & hat. The roadster show was two months before the near fatal accident.

At the roadster show one of the booths was an insurance booth and we talked about auto insurance for classic cars. We had never had a classic auto policy on our Thunderbird. He looked at our car and said we definitely needed classic insurance on it so I made an appointment and ***we purchased a policy which took effect on May 1, 2016, two weeks before the accident.***

How did God direct the happenings before and after May 14, 2016?

- We had automobile insurance and for most people it would have been satisfactory but it was not designed for a car that was a one of a kind fifty-seven year old classic automobile but we had everyday normal insurance on it for thirty years so most people would think why change?

- But *when God speaks you need to listen.* We went to a car show like so many before but I stopped by an insurance booth which would be the last booth I would normally go to since we already had insurance on our vehicles, but I had an inner voice speaking to me and I listened.

- Everyone has an inner voice but not everyone pays attention. If you pray on a daily basis God will speak to you and you will be in tune to your inner voice.

- I made the insurance appointment, changed insurance on the thunderbird and it was in effect on May 1, 2016. The accident was May 14, 2016. If we had not had that policy there would not have been enough insurance to cover Ron's medical bills and get a safe car that would protect him.

- The paramedics didn't think there could be a survivor in the rubble of the Thunderbird but they didn't understand that the *"Miracle of God"* was at work.

- It could have turned out so differently if we didn't have a miracle that began so much earlier. God knew what was going to happen that spring day, long before the day arrived, and he was orchestrating our life to protect an eighty-one-year-old man that was on blood thinners so that his beloved award-winning trophy didn't become his final resting place.

Now would be a perfect time for everyone to start believing in *"Miracles."*

After the accident our insurance agent said the company would take care of us, not to worry about it, but if we had an attorney, they wouldn't be able to talk to us.

The attorney we hired to help us with Progressive Insurance and the Cisneros driver and grandpa case decided they weren't worth his time when he discovered we had a $250,000/uninsured/underinsured policy.

Why go for hamburger when you can have prime rib. The Dietzler's Insurance company would be a much larger PAYDAY for him so he forced his services by filing a lien against our insurance company. He received between $93,000 and $100,000 for one deposition and filing a lien. **Not bad for a day's work!**

It won't help going to the Bar Association. I tried that and they are attorney's that look out for the attorneys so you can plan on them being biased because they hang out together, play golf and will not be objective.

So, the best thing is to pray that you get a good attorney that is honest and has integrity.

I hired the attorney to deal with Oscar Cisneros and his Grandpa and their insurance company. We didn't discuss anything about our insurance. *I did not hire him to work with our company because everything was going smoothly.* **I didn't discuss or mention anything about our insurance company. It was not part of our conversation and I never requested that he make contact with them**.

I didn't realize there was a problem until we got his recommendation. At that point I discovered his recommendation was tied to both Oscar's grandpa's insurance company and to our insurance company because that was where the **BIG PAY CHECK** was going to be for our attorney. **He decided not to pursue Oscar or his grandpa and only accept the $25,000 from Progressive Insurance as their final settlement.**

Our Attorney had been recommended to me and his website says that he is *aaggressive, successful* and *dedicated* and that is all true but he goes after his own client, not the opposing client. *He decided that Oscar and his grandpa wasn't worth his time and effort* but that there was a potential large payday if he concentrated on our insurance company, so **he filed a lien against them and wouldn't release the lien unless we kept him on as our attorney.**

We were left with no choice but to keep the attorney because he had made it impossible for us to get any money to pay for the rising expenses from the accident if we didn't get the insurance settlement.

Did I like being backed into a corner by the law firm? No, but we were already under so much stress that we just wanted to get the case settled. Would I ever recommend the attorney that we used to anyone else that was desperate to find a compassionate, caring, dedicated law firm? Absolutely Not! This attorney will go after the money under whatever rock he can find it, even if it happens to benefit the firm and hurt his client.

The good news:

We survived the attorney with his huge settlement from our insurance company that he didn't deserve.

- Ron is slowly healing from his wounds but still misses his thunderbird.

- We were able to get a Subaru Impreza with a ton of safety features to help protect Ron when he is in a car.

- We have not been able to find a classic car that can replace the one of a kind Thunderbird that Oscar left as a death trap on the freeway that early morning in May, but

- Ron lived to see his beloved Chicago Cubs win the world series Sept.20 (four months after Oscar drank, drove at a high rate of speed, fell asleep, & hit a fifty-seven-year-old award-winning Thunderbird and left an eighty-one-year old upside down on the highway trapped inside in critical condition)

Oscar probably never owned anything that he valued, that would cause him pain & anguish if he lost it or it was destroyed so chances are, he didn't give the auto accident, that almost killed my husband and destroyed a beautiful classic trophy that he adored a second thought.

But what he doesn't realize is *"The choices we make today **WILL** affect all of our **TOMORROWS!***

- The police report will follow him

- This book will follow him

- Facebook will follow him

- Social Media will follow him

We need to choose wisely because our choices will follow us.

This picture is Ron's final farewell to his beloved Thunderbird!

Christmas Surprise
(God's Touch)

You would have thought he had won the lottery when he saw that car. The man that shows little emotion was like a kid that was going to get to spend the night in a candy store. To this day I am amazed that he didn't spend the night in the TBird. With his excitement I am sure the cool leather seats could have kept him warm in the twenty-three-degree winter snowy night.

What did he do with his new play toy? First of all, you need a CHEERING SECTION so he put an ad in the Idaho Statesman announcing there was a new car club in town, posters on bulletin boards, and he joined the National Heartland Thunderbird Club. He was off and running with approximately thirty eager potential new members at his first meeting and he was the President of the club for the first ten years leading the way too many trophy winning car shows all across the Treasure Valley.

Over the past thirty years Ron's 1959 Thunderbird won over fifty trophies and numerous plaques. In the spring and summer, he would shine and polish his car and off he would go to a car show.

At Christmas the Third was always in the holiday parade and many times it would carry the wedding party from the church to a reception.

I often wonder what lessons, if any, that Oscar Cisneros, who decided to drink and drive may have learned that fateful night and early morning in 2016. Did he ever have any regrets? Would he like a do-over? Did he or his grandpa learn anything that day? If they did learn a lesson, or found a church, or prayed for forgiveness. If they are learning how to give to others, maybe, just maybe, it will be worth watching the sadness in my husband's eyes when he sees pictures of his beloved Thunderbird, or when he looks at the farewell picture when I took him out to say a final "Goodbye" to the Thunderbird.

Or the sadness he feels when thinks about no longer going to the Third Club meetings that he started because he doesn't own a Thunderbird any more.

My husband almost had his beloved TBird as his final resting place on the freeway and he still has not totally recovered from being hit by a drunk driver, while Oscar continues his life as if he doesn't have a care in the world.

True…….I'm sorry does go a long way to heal a heart but is seldom used

Tragedy, Tears, Sadness, Loss, Brings God's Gift.

LESSON # 02
Pick & Choose Your Battles Wisely.
Don't Make Every Situation A Battleground.
Do Everything with Integrity, Honesty & Principle.

Ron and I decided to move to an over 55 community. I have been working my business part time and volunteering with a couple of non-profit organizations plus I would leave on occasions and have lunch, play cards with friends, or have events at our church. I wanted a safe environment for Ron in case he had a problem I wanted to make sure there were people around him he could call on for help so we began looking at over 55 communities because they always had activities and people that had similar interests.

We found a great community of 116 homes and selected one of the last homes to be built. We began the process and started packing boxes. It was difficult because Ron didn't have much energy and was limited on what he could do so I basically asked him to pack his clothes when it was time and pack his items in the garage and I would take care of the rest. Early on I was in my closet on a step ladder getting a heavy box of shoes off of a shelf when I fell backwards and hit my head on the top of the toilet and my back on the bottom of the toilet. I crawled out of the bathroom shouting for Ron for help and he finally came to see what the commotion was all about. I had him check me out and he said I had a large bruise on my left hip.

I made a Doctor's appointment to have it checked out and was told I had a concussion and there were bulging discs in my lower back. I was scheduled with a neurologist for brain testing and physical therapy for my lower back. I was instructed to rest my brain until it had a chance to heal and the physical therapy would help strengthen my back. We were packing boxes and getting ready to move in the next ninety days and there was so much to do that it was difficult for me to take the time to rest my body, let alone my brain.

I called both sons and asked them if they could take the time to stop by and give me a hand. Tyson stopped by one day to go up in the attic and toss some boxes down to me before he was off again on his Uber run for his second job as a taxi driver. I asked Paul to drop by and help me change out some light fixtures that I had purchased so we could take our special-order fixtures we had in the great room and bedroom with us to our new home but he said he didn't have time so I hired someone to do the job. Still unable to rest my brain I packed boxes. Ron helped put them on a hand truck and I put all of the boxes in the garage including all of the furniture with the exception of the large items.

Our friends also helped install an attic ladder so we could store the empty boxes and they have helped us along the way. Ron has tried to be helpful but the auto accident took so much out of him that I try not to ask very much of him because I can tell how little energy he has and I am so grateful to have him with me because he is my best friend and I don't want to do anything that can shorten the length of time my best friend is with me.

When our house was built for some reason it was on a 9% grade from the front of the house to the rear of the house. I noticed that other builders would grade the entire lot before they would start the foundation. Our builder graded only the area where he planned on building the house, not the entire lot, so the rest of the lot was not completely flat when they started the foundation.

One evening my husband and I dropped by the lot after the house was framed. The back patio and front porch were completed. When I walked out the back door, I noticed an immediate problem. There was approximately a two-foot drop from the back door to the patio. There should normally be a very small step when you walk out the back door.

I called and the Forman stopped by to take a look at the situation. His solution was to put two LARGE STEPS as you come out the back door which I immediately vetoed. This is a senior community and I could see a multitude of liability issues with that solution, considering many seniors had canes, walkers, have bad knees, bad hips and poor eyesight.

In addition, the lighting supplier had planned on putting a light with a fan on the patio that would cool people as they came out the door and stood on the two steps but it would be totally useless to anyone sitting at the patio table unless you hired someone to blow the breeze from the fan in their direction.

They finally decided to make the patio two feet tall from the ground so it will be even with the edge of the back door, (That is a lot of concrete) and bring in dirt to make it even with the patio. I did end up with a two-foot-high patio which now meant the six-foot privacy fence was useless because when you are on the patio and the neighbors are on their patio you are eye ball to eyeball.........NO PRIVACY.

I would love to have the privacy; however, it was more important to me that my clients and friends were safe. I explained to the builder that when you have a patio made of concrete, two feet off the ground in a senior community, it is creating a potential liability problem for friends, neighbors and clients that might go onto the patio. I said that all of his other homes in the community have a patio that is ground level and since my patio is not ground level, he needs to put a rod iron fence on the patio to match the front porch so that chairs won't slide off and people have something to hold on to for safety.

They didn't commit to the fence until there was an accident. I was carrying a stainless-steel editing machine and slipped on the concrete, hit my head on the house, caught the editing machine with my face. I hit both my head and my back and was dazed but my concern at the time was my mangled eyeglasses. I tried to fix them the best I could but the next morning I went to the eye doctor to get them fixed properly.

His first comment was "Did you go to the Emergency Room?" I said no. He said "You need to go and get checked out. You could have a brain bleed." So off to the hospital I went for an MRI. This time I had an MRI, talked to the radiologist, and went to see the Neurologist. He said I had a double concussion which also caused a traumatic brain injury and a back and hip injury. He said if I was a football player, he would tell me my football playing days are over. I have been in therapy ever since.

I was told I needed to rest my brain, do not try to multi-task, and give it a chance to heal. I am trying but I am not sure I know how to do nothing. I will be filling out a form and have to ask my husband a simple question like "What's our address?"

Remember I have had three concussions in a matter of four months. It scares me so much not to remember things because I am so fiercely independent and to know that Ron and I have to rely on just each other.

When I first had trouble forgetting addresses, names or bits of information I was worried it was a form of dementia but I didn't tell anyone but my doctor assures me my brain just needs to heal and it will take time.

I have a client that lives close by that has a genetic disorder and sometimes she is so sick that she is bedridden for months, then she will be fine for several years. Not long ago I found out that her husband has early onset Alzheimer's and it doesn't appear that they have family that is available to help out so they have around the clock help taking care of them. That is so sad. Not many people can afford that kind of twenty-four-hour care.

I had another friend, Bev Ross, that was in Soroptimist with me who was a Real Estate Broker and smart as a whip. She developed Alzheimer's when she was around sixty-five. She didn't have the disease long before she passed away. I think of her often. She helped me with one of my real estate transactions. I only did business with people that I felt were honest with integrity and she was one of the best.

All those memories flood through me when I have the split-second memory lapses and I get worried, even though the neurologist said I just need to give my brain the time to heal and I must admit I am not doing a very good job of resting it. But then I go to Red Hat game day or luncheon and everyone there seems to have a memory problem so I laugh and think to myself "my brain isn't so messed up after all, I'll just hang out with these crazy ladies more often and I'll feel even better about myself."

But through everything, God preformed a miracle. He gave us a mortgage company that was excellent with finances and they helped us take the money the lawyer left us with in the end and use it for the down payment, closing costs and real estate fees for our new home in an over 55 community, Ron and PePe take long walks in their neighborhood every day and visit with their friends.

We have a rock in front of our house that says "Welcome to our little corner of the world which was born out of sorrow, pain and loss. May all who enter be blessed with a Miracle." A picture of the Thunderbird is on the rock.

CHAPTER 2

PAINFUL PAST/SHATTERED LEGACY

Painful Memory #1

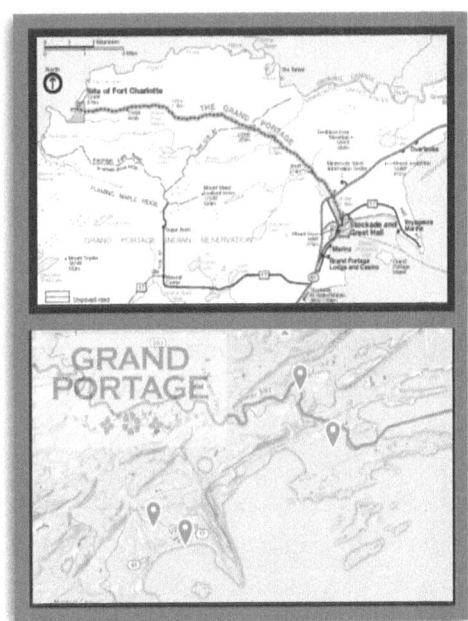

I was approximately thirty years old when one of the most traumatic heartbreaking chapters of my life occurred. I had never called on God more for his help during my life than I did for the solid year that my son was missing and I had no idea where he was or if I would ever see him again.

I was newly married for the second time. My son had been kidnapped by his Dad for nearly a year and I had no idea where he was. I spent months writing letters, making phone calls and on my knees praying for guidance. One night while I was on my knees, my prayer changed. Instead of praying that I would get my son back I prayed that God please show me what he wanted for my son.

If he wanted my son to remain with his Dad, I prayed that he would show me a sign so I would stop pursuing the search and I could learn to live without him. The very next day I received a phone call from the Wichita, Kansas Police Department telling me I could go to Grand Portage, Minnesota, which is right next to the Canadian border, and pick up my son. God was guiding me during the year long ordeal and watching over my son. *(An Everyday Miracle)*

The next problem, however, was that I had no money to make the trip so I drove to my Dad's house and asked him if I could borrow the money so I could go get my five-year-old son. He loaned me the funds and my new husband and I left for Minnesota.

By the time we arrived at our destination it was late in the evening and we were very tired. We found the Sheriff and the Counselor that had placed my son with a family until we could pick him up. The Counselor instructed us to not spend the night in the town after we picked up my son. He said it was not safe. He told us to keep driving until we reached the center part of the state before stopping to rest. We were followed for many miles before we no longer saw headlights in the rear-view mirror.

But there was an emotional price to pay. My small son threw-up most of the evening and part of the next day. It is hard on a child when they see tension between their parents and they sometimes think they might be the reason for the tension. Seldom is that true and in our case it definitely wasn't true. His Dad and I both loved him.

That was never in question. If my son's Dad had realized that we knew his location he could have easily traveled to Canada and disappeared. If that had happened, I may have never seen my son again. After returning to Wichita, Kansas I knew I needed to change careers. I was working 8:00 am - 6:00 pm and my son was in school for 1/2 a day. He was my top priority so I needed to find a job that I could work around my son's school schedule.

From the time Tyson was returned to me I was committed to always be home when he got home from school and to never have a job or business that took me away from my family and I kept that promise. I was able to participate in school functions, and I was Tyson's Cub Scout den leader and always helped with his school functions and boy scouts. I also participated with him in Optimist football and other activities he might be interested in. He was very good at selling items to win prizes. I was able to be a stay at home mom because I was a Sales Director with Mary Kay Cosmetics.

Painful Memory #2
The men in my life...and the lessons that followed.

The first male that I remember was my step-dad but I didn't know that he wasn't my birth Dad until I was sixteen. He was usually a very soft spoken, hardworking, easy going and kind hearted dad. I remember him cooking, helping me with my homework, and making snow forts. He never raised his voice or laid a hand on me until I was sixteen years old when I found out that I was adopted.

My mother enraged him to the point that he picked up a belt and beat me until I not only had welts, he split my lip open with the belt before he stopped. After my brother and sisters were born my bedroom was moved to the basement and in the middle of the night my dad would slip down to the basement and sexually abuse me. I would pretend to be asleep but it didn't stop him. He continued to do it nightly after everyone was in bed.

I didn't have anyone I could turn to for help and I didn't want to do anything that would cause problems for the only person that had loved me up to this point in my life. I was so traumatized that I don't even know when the abuse began.

I only know that it was happening until I made the decision to leave home. But I never held it against him for some reason because I saw how terrible my mother treated him and I didn't know how anyone could be so mean to another human being.

Daddy was in the hospital after having a heart attack when he found out my mother had told the hospital staff not to let me in to see him. He got so mad and tried to get out of bed to come out in the hall and tell the nurses to let me in his room when he suddenly had another heart attack and this time he didn't recover, he died.

I was is the waiting room and didn't get to see him for the previous three days and didn't get to see him before he passed away even though I was only a few feet away.

Within fifteen minutes my mother was on the phone in the hospital waiting room, not interested in what she needed to do for my dad, but where was the money and how much would she get.

Every summer my mother sent me to Fredonia, Kansas to spend the summer with my grandparents. I liked spending time with my grandma. She taught me things about cooking and baking. They didn't have a bathroom so you went to the bathroom in an outhouse attached to the chicken coop and you took a bath in a large tin tub on the back porch.

I absolutely hated the outhouse and tub. I would have loved my grandpa too except he was my second encounter with sexual abuse. I have blocked out most of my visits that I had with my grandparents but I remember how the problem started. My grandpa would ask me to sit on his lap facing him and he would sexually abuse me. Every summer I asked my parents not to send me to Fredonia to no avail. Every summer I went to my dreaded sexual camp.

After I left home, I graduated from high school, dated a lot, was engaged twice but broke one off and one of them broke it off with me, then I met the next significant man in my life.

I had two sets of parents. When I was young, I only knew about one set of parents but there was another set that could have been part of my life.

I never held the abuse I received from my step-dad against him because I also remembered everything he did for me when I was a little girl. I knew that my mother never did anything with me as a child or as a teenager.

When we look at our life, we only see what is immediately in front of our eyes but God sees the entire picture and he knows what has happened and what will happen in our future.

My birth Dad had three other children and his wife drank and did drugs. My Dad didn't use any drugs as far as I knew but that didn't matter because his wife got her own children started on drugs and addicted to them.

In the end his only son got shot by either a family member or he shot himself. There seemed to be a problem with the details of the final report as to what really happened.

I would have had a huge family to get to know and love if I had the opportunity to be part of their family and I am sad I missed out on the closeness of family. I might have had someone looking out for me along the way.

But I couldn't have had a better protector that God on my side... I had to learn that men are not always doing what is best for me but ***I believe God gave me the best home under the circumstances.***

If I had not learned there is a God, how to pray, and that I wasn't alone I am not sure I would have survived.

Painful Memory #3
When Mother Walked Out, God Walked In.

Lesson #03
*Only you give your past Power.....*Oprah

When my Dad died, I was left with the childhood emotional trauma and pain that I had not been able to heal and I was acting out the pain by getting even through smoking. My Dad was a smoker and now that he was gone, I would never be able to hear an apology from him for abusing me when I was growing up nor would I be able to lash out at him.

I graduated from high school and decided to go to California but the only job I could find was selling used cars in a dealership in San Diego during the day and at night I sang part time in a night club. It was going fairly well but I wasn't making much money and I was living in a motel which was costing a fortune.

My boss was forty years old and I was eighteen but he asked to marry me and I told him I would think about it. I finally decided to go back to Kansas but I didn't have the money so I called my mother to see if she would send me money for a train ticket and she said no and hung up on me. I was so depressed that I overdosed on sleeping pills and cleaning fluid. The motel maid found me and I was rushed to the hospital.

Two weeks later, after I started to improve and the doctors talked about releasing me, I called my mother again to see if she would send me money and once again, she said no and said "She didn't want me back" and hung up.

My boss came to the hospital and picked me up, bought me a ticket to fly home and said if once I got home, I decided I wanted to come back to him in California just call and he would send me a ticket to fly back.

I think he knew that once I was on familiar ground I wouldn't be back.

After I got back to Kansas, I got a job at Wesley Medical Center and I would like to say that it was smooth sailing the rest of the way but not quite. I worked at the hospital and while working there I met my first Love.

First Love
What Happened to First Love?

How do you deal with the pain of losing your "First Love and a baby?"

Everyone should sit down to write a book. You will eventually remember things whether you want to or not, at least bits and pieces. I realize, now more than ever, the importance of keeping notes and a journal of things that are happening on a daily basis so you don't have to try and re-create it years later. Google has recently become my best friend as I piece together and weave the pieces of my life in order to try and make sense of the past seventy years.

I don't know how I could have forgotten my very first engagement. I was nineteen years old when I met Larry Huckleberry.

I was working at Wesley Medical Center and lived across the street from the hospital where I was renting a room.

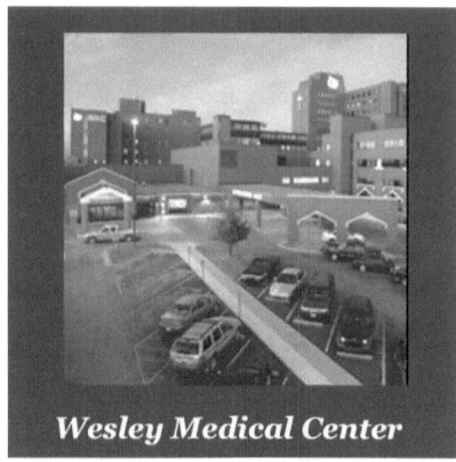

Wesley Medical Center

I don't remember how I met him. Both him and his brother were avid water skiers. He was so good that he even skied barefoot. One of his biggest challenges was probably when he taught me to water ski. I think it probably took at least three months to get me up on skis. It didn't help that they decided to teach me in the dead of winter when it must have been not more than twenty-five degrees outside with snow on the ground.

We dated six months when he asked me to marry him and we planned on a June wedding. We spent every free moment water skiing. But something went wrong and I have no idea what. Maybe he decided he wasn't ready for marriage. It will always remain a mystery.

Larry was supposed to call me so we could make arrangements to go to his cabin and water ski for the weekend. I didn't receive any calls that weekend and I didn't receive and calls the next week so I decided to do something I normally would never do.

I called my Dad and asked him if he would drive me to Larry's cabin so I could find out what was going on since I didn't own a car.

He drove me out to the lake and when we arrived, I walked in the cabin door and Larry was taking a nap on the bed. He woke up and I asked him if there was something wrong. I said I was confused because he hasn't called and I didn't have any idea what is going on.

He said he wasn't sure what he wanted and he didn't call because he didn't know how to tell me that he just wasn't ready to get married.

I was so devastated because he didn't have the guts to call me & I had to pry it out of him so I threw his engagement ring at him & walked out. That was the last time I saw him.

I went back to work still in pain from my break-up with Larry when one of my friends from Wesley Medical Center asked me to go out for a drink with a group after our 11:00 pm shift ended. I usually didn't go out because I was never much of a night owl since I was so shy but I decided to go. I had one drink and that was the last thing I remember.

I woke up in a strange apartment complex dazed and confused, with no clothes on, with several men all passed out, and all I wanted was to get dressed and get out of there and home safely. I quietly got dressed and slipped out the door trying not to wake anyone and ran as fast as I could down the street and kept running until I managed to get back to the room I was renting so I could feel safe.

I now had to deal with the pain from the break-up from my first love and I had a pain so unimaginable to deal with, *a gang rape by men I didn't know*, didn't remember, and was given *a drug that blocked my memory*. *Those two incidents affected my future relationships not only with men but all relationships throughout my life including my ability to trust.*

I am sure that Larry Huckleberry probably went on with his life without a care in the world after he broke up with me without so much as a conversation, not realizing the devastation he left behind from his careless choices. *We must always remember each decision we make has consequences,* some good, some bad. He left a trail of destruction that followed me for decades without me understanding the reasons behind the pain and heartache.

I came from an abusive childhood before I met Larry and without warning he walked out of my life without so much as a word, two days later I was gang raped and drugged and four months later found out I was pregnant by either a person that didn't deserve me or by a rapist. It verified my greatest fear; **ALL MEN ARE ABUSIVE. DON'T TRUST THEM.** It is amazing I kept my sanity.

There were many things that happened during my childhood, teen and young adult years that were so traumatic that I remember only bits and pieces or they have been totally blocked out consciously but even if I can't recall the memories that happened they still left a permanent imprint on my mind and my life and they affected all future relationships and decisions.

When love is replaced by violence it damages the heart and soul. You may be able to find ways to ease the pain but you will never be able to completely erase the memory.

I have not shared my story with anyone until now because if you have not been violated in such a cruel way you can't possibly understand the fear that a victim feels.

Family & friends think you should just get over it. It is over! Stop thinking about it!

Let it go! It's not that easy. Something was taken from you without your permission.

In my case, ***I lost my memory and almost lost my ability to have children forever.***

My memory started to come back because of the Judge Kavanaugh nomination confirmation hearings for the Supreme Court. If I had not started writing my book in July, 2018 perhaps, I would not have started remembering the past. It probably began with the election of our current

President, who had been in the news so much due to the many harassment cases from women, and with the trial and conviction of Bill Cosby.

It seemed like every time I turned on the news there was another Senator, Movie Star or someone else notable that was being accused of sexual harassment so I thought about it but I didn't think in terms of it affecting me until I heard Christine Blasey Ford's story and the precautions she has taken to feel safe. Her story triggered my memories. All of the memories were present but it was as if I had just had eye surgery and suddenly, I was able to understand what happened that horrible night fifty-five years ago

Once I started writing my life story my thoughts drifted back to the years I had blocked out.

As I put down the information that I remembered suddenly I started filling in the blanks on the page with information as the pieces of the puzzle started to come together. I remembered the pain from the sudden break-up with my fiancée' two days earlier without any warning.

I remembered going to work at Wesley Medical Center that Friday and my co-workers asked me to go to a local pub for a drink after we got off work.

Then I started asking questions out loud: ***"Why don't I remember anything after I had the first two sips of my drink?"***

What happened to cause me to forget?"

Then I remembered! Right after we got to the pub, I ordered my drink but then I went to the restroom. When I got back my drink was on the table and I sat down and started to sip on it. That was the last thing I remember until I woke up in a strange location, with strange men.

All I could think about was getting out of there and getting to the safety of my rooming house. I know I started walking as fast as I could. I don't remember if I walked all the way home or if I called a cab. I didn't have a cell phone. You didn't have cell phones in 1964.

I should have looked up at the address, called the police and filed charges but my brain was so foggy that I couldn't make sense of anything that happened. I was so naive that until I started writing this book, I was unable to put the pieces together.

The more I typed my story, the more questions I had but as I was working on my book, I was watching the Kavanaugh Senate hearing and I also listened to Michael Avenatti, who was representing one of the Kavanaugh accusers. While listening to him I was suddenly able to put all of the pieces of my life together that summer night in 1964. I learned that there is no statute of limitations for "rape" but I don't know where it happened or who did it so my situation is different and will probably always be unsolved.

Fifty-five years later, everything now makes sense. I now realize why I couldn't remember anything that happened that night. ***It is because I had been given a date rape drug that night.*** I was so naive, I dated very little in high school and didn't date very much after graduation. In addition, I had never heard of "date rape drugs."

What happened that night? ***I was drugged and gang raped!*** The drugs & trauma caused me to block the memory of the event for fifty-five years.

That night changed my life. I didn't know I was pregnant until the baby aborted four months later and I was told I probably would never have any more children because I developed a severe infection. I never had consistent periods so between the rape and stress I didn't think about the possibility of a pregnancy.

I don't know if the pregnancy was from the night of the gang rape or from my first love Larry who broke up with me two days earlier. I did finally have a son a few years later but I was never able to have any more children.

Because of that night I was never able to trust people, especially men so it has been difficult for me to develop close friendships. If this ever happens to you don't keep quiet and don't ever think it was your fault.

I don't feel a man can possibly come close to knowing how you can feel if you have been harassed or raped. If you don't believe me just look at the Judiciary Confirmation hearings. They didn't have a clue, not even the women.

Even some of my female friends don't come close to understanding how a victim feels. I know because when they talked about the Kavanaugh hearings their sympathy was with the Judge who showed anger and disdain, not compassion for the victim of so many years earlier. If you take the potential rape and harassment out of the picture, the judge doesn't have the temperament to be on the highest court in the land.

If Judge Kavanaugh's alcohol consumption isn't a problem, if he didn't try to rape Christine Blasey Ford and he only wanted to protect his reputation why did he show such anger. Don't Judges know how to control their emotions, temper and anger?

If what he was saying was truthful, he could have put the issue to rest by taking a lie detector test and releasing the results to the public.

I know how she must have felt because I have been in similar shoes. It takes guts to tell a story of harassment, abuse or rape as a woman. Women need to support women that have been violated. Rape and sexual harassment are not a Republican or Democratic issue. It is a Right and Wrong issue. Absolutely no question about it.

I have many friends that are making similar comments as the white male Senators and female Senators are making about Judge Kavanaugh and Christine Blasey Ford. So, I know that if they don't show any type of compassion for her, they can't possibly show compassion or love for me if they knew my story. It is so sad when party is more important than principles & friendship. I can't imagine what it is like to carry this type of burden without the support of friends and family, but I am sure she lost friends because of her story and so will I.

They were so determined to get him confirmed to the Supreme Court that they ignored common sense, didn't listen to facts, or allow the FBI to interview people that can help them get the answers they need to make the right decision.

I believe Brett Kavanaugh sexually assaulted Christine Blasey Ford in high school and the 2018 United States Senate allowed him to do it a second time by not doing a complete investigation.

I immediately knew the strength of Christine Blasey Ford's credibility the moment I heard she had a second "escape door" added to her new home in 2012 because *abused women take precautions* that is a foreign concept to a person that has not been involved in violence.

The Senators seem to have conflicting views about what they believe about sexual harassment, rape accusations, and domestic violence among people that work in Washington DC. Some of the Representatives and Senators have been put in positions they had to resign and fade into the sunset while others that were accused, with alleged proof, went on the be confirmed to the Supreme Court or become President of the United States.

Whether you are violated by the anger and pain from domestic violence, rape, sexual or verbal abuse it will still influence your future decisions and relationships. **Principles and doing what is right should always trump politics** but that sentiment probably will never reach Washington DC, at least not in this administration. I don't know if it is possible in any administration. I have heard the President; First Lady and the Senate make the following comment:

"She can't be telling the truth…She doesn't remember the exact date, time, place, and location of the encounter. So, you can't believe her." *I can understand why they would say that!*

Someone probably never attempted to rape them. Ask someone like me.

I can't answer any of those questions either and I wasn't able to put together the details of my gang-rape for fifty-five years. That doesn't mean I was lying. It means I was traumatized and so was she.

Judge Kavanaugh stated *"What goes around comes around." I hope there is complete truth in that statement and I believe there is.*

Each of us has been give the ability to make choices. Maybe someday Congress will make decisions based on **PRINCIPLES** not **PARTY.**

Choose to do what is right instead of what is popular. (Don't run with the crowd. Stand above them and make a statement.)

What All Women Need To Know about date-rape drugs:

What Is A Date-Rape Drug?

When a date rape drug begins to cause symptoms and how long they last depend on how much you are given and whether it's mixed with alcohol or other drugs. *Alcohol can make the effects even stronger. Symptoms of date rape drugs generally include dizziness, confusion, and loss of memory.*

Date rape drugs are powerful.
drowsiness and dizziness
vision problems
feelings of relaxation
Increased sensuality
seizures
memory loss
sweating
slow heart rate
nausea and vomiting
blackouts
loss of consciousness
slurred speech
feeling very drunk, even if you've only had one drink
loss of muscle control
confusion
lowered blood pressure

How can you protect yourself from date rape drugs?

don't take drinks from other people

open containers yourself

watch your drink being poured or mixed at a bar and carry it yourself

if you need to go to the bathroom, take your drink with you; if you can't, leave it with a trusted friend

don't drink anything that tastes or smells odd

if you've left your drink unattended, pour it out

if you feel very drunk after you only had a small amount of alcohol, or none at all, seek help right away

Keep in mind that alcohol in large doses can also make someone unconscious and unable to defend themselves. Recognizing the symptoms of date rape drugs and keeping an eye out for intoxicated friends can go a long way.

Here are a few stories to illustrate my point about how rape can alter the course of a woman's life forever.

The names of the survivor stores have been changed to protect their privacy.

Story #1
Rape steals women's career before it gets started

Mary was a freshman student when she was raped and almost immediately dropped out of college. Her assailant was a stranger, who turned out to be a stalker. She had been sitting outside her house one night having some milk and cookies when, she felt like she was falling off the porch, but she wasn't falling. Someone had grabbed her from behind.

She was dragged under a neighbor's porch. He assaulted her in many different ways, and she thought he was going to kill her. Her education stopped at that moment. She first worked with the college to change her ID and stay enrolled, but her attacker managed to reach her by phone.

Frightened, she left school and she married soon after, allowing her identity to fade into that of her husband's as she followed him around the country for his career. She felt like, the more invisible she could be, just be Steve's wife, it'd be safer. But she dreaded the moments at parties when Steve's accomplished friends turned to her to ask, "And what do you do?"

She held jobs as a nanny in several cities, and learned to manage despite her nightmares and anxiety attacks. Before the rape, she had planned to become a nurse. Giving up on that made her feel "like a failure," she says. She wondered to herself, "Why couldn't I just get over this?"

After her assailant, a serial rapist, was finally captured and imprisoned in 2011, partly with evidence from Mary's rape kit, ***she became an advocate for victims' rights.***

Story #2
Becoming Enough - A Survivor's Story

In the spring of 2012, a college student's innocence became her biggest mistake and her greatest flaw when she met the most honest-looking blonde boy at a school pre-game party at a local bar.

At some point they start dancing and he lets her have his drink. They keep dancing and she starts forgetting. Her next memory is he is walking her down the street and into her dorm room. Her memory is blank and she vaguely remembers the blonde boy on top of her.

She remembers saying no, I'm a virgin but he doesn't pay any attention to her protest. He yelled that she was too tight but continued to assault her, ignoring her muffled protests.

The next morning, she woke up, dazed, confused, and bloody but her college assailant was gone. The rape changed her life in many ways but she survived to go on and help other women that have had similar experiences. She has realized the positive changes she has made since the rape but is wasn't easy.

She will never be the same person as she was before and some of the repercussions seem cruel; however, she has become more confident. She got involved in a support group with other women who have been raped and was able to finally comprehend that nothing she did was her fault.

Here is what I believe about her story: I believe that the same thing happened to her that happened to me so many years ago. I believe she was given a date rape drug so that it would be easy for the guy to rape her without her fighting him off. That is why she had the lapses in her memory.

"True Bravery Is Doing What Is Right Even When It's Not Popular!" When she wrote her story, here is what she had to say:

To my rapist's friend who knew that he had put something in my drink and didn't say anything: you didn't rape me but you helped my perpetrator.

To the many friends I lost: I'm sorry you couldn't deal with me when I needed you the most.

To the friends who have been more supportive than I could ever imagine: thank you. You're the reason I'm still here.

And to my rapist: you didn't win that night. You might have taken my virginity and changed my perspective on life but I am stronger because of you.

Lastly and most importantly, to all of my fellow survivors, because you are a survivor, not a victim: I believe you. You are enough. You are not alone.

Story #3
One more story I will share:

A woman we will call Sue, who is a 33-year-old project manager has taken over a decade to get over a truly horrific ordeal at the hands of a so-called 'friend. She was out with friends at a local pub when one of her friends that she saw daily at the gym asked to tag along with her friends for a few drinks. She popped in to the restroom, leaving her drink "safe' with her friends and on her return, finished her second drink. That's when her fun evening began to turn into an actual living nightmare.

She now knows that at some point – presumably while she was in the toilet – ***her drink was spiked with Rohypnol. (Rohypnol is the date rape drug that's used as a hypnotic, sedative, anticonvulsant, anxiolytic***

and skeletal muscle relaxant). What happened next is extremely hazy in her mind – it felt like a movie edit was occurring before her eyes each time she blinked.

She had gone to the toilet and collapsed. She was hanging on to the basin for dear life when a bouncer came inside and took her outside for fresh air, presuming she was drunk. But by then, she only had two drinks. The next thing she knew, her gym friend was beside her, and they were in a cab.

He took her to her home and by then. the drug had now taken full control of her and her memories are just a series of flashbacks. He raped her many times over throughout the night and early morning. In the morning she went to the toilet and was violently sick and also noticed she was bleeding from her rectum but couldn't understand why. It was then he raped her again before he finished and left.

The experience was so devastating that she ended up losing her job because she was afraid to leave her house. It has now been ten years since that fateful day and each year has gradually got easier. Her life is back on track and she has refused to let an animal like him destroy her. You may not forget the incident, but you can control it and not let the rapist win. To all of the victims of attempted rape, rape, verbal/no-verbal abuse, domestic violence who think you are alone and have no voice: You are not alone! There are many women across the nation that know what you have gone through because we have been there.

I would have loved to have a little girl but I am not sure if I could have handled it knowing the circumstances, not sure if it belonged to Larry Huckleberry or a rapist. I would have never been in that situation if I hadn't been so torn apart over my sudden breakup.

I have told my clients that you will remember things from your past when you are ready to handle it and, in my case, it took fifty-five years before I could remember what happened and a confirmation hearing for a Supreme Court Justice in order for me to start the painful journey.

If you are a woman and have not experienced any type of harassment or abuse congratulations, but that doesn't let you off the hook. It is your responsibility to be a united voice for ALL WOMEN that need your help, not just me.

For the women that turned their back on Christine Blasey Ford's plea for you to rally beside her I feel sorry for you. There comes a time in a person's life that you need to put Principles ahead of Party, but first we need to elect people that have Principles.

"What can I say! I thought I was alone but God was walking beside me through so much trauma. I could have died when I overdosed in California but God intervened. (A Miracle) When my Mother once again abandoned me, I could have made the wrong choice and married a man because I had nowhere else to turn but instead, I was given the option to return home so I could have a chance to get back on my feet". (Another Miracle)

I got a job at Wesley Medical Center in Wichita, Kansas, found a room in a boarding house across from the hospital where I worked for about a year when I met my first love, Larry Huckleberry. I went out for a drink with co-workers and that was the last thing I remember but as bad as things went that night it could have been worse; I could have lost my life.

I had no idea where I was or how I got there when I opened my eyes, dazed and in a fog and scared. All I knew was I needed to get out of there before they woke up and attacked me again. I got dressed, out the door and somehow, I got home safely. (God's Miracle)

The drugs and trauma caused me to not remember the event and I was shocked when I found out I was aborting a baby since I wasn't dating but I was also relieved because ***I wasn't prepared to be a mom. I was barely supporting myself at the moment. Once again, a Miracle happened.*** I was protected the night I went out with the hospital employees. ***God protected me so that I was able to get home safely. (Miracle)***

Since the child would have been from a traumatic event, I feel God was protecting the fetus and me from future pain and hardship. (Miracle)

It is hard enough to make it in this world without stacking the deck against you. Both of us went through trauma that night and we didn't need any more trauma.

Many people say that the baby could have been born and then adopted but when a baby is born from such a traumatizing event not only the mother remembers the event but the fetus feels the emotions of the event and it also affects their future life events as well.

No one at work ever said anything after the night we went out so I didn't know if any of them were involved in the rape because all I wanted to do was get out of the place because there were naked bodies everywhere and I didn't immediately recognize any of them.

I wasn't able to put the pieces of the puzzle of what happened that night together until I started writing my manuscript.

When I heard the Kavanaugh hearings and Christine Blasey Ford's said that she added a second escape door to her new house she built in 2012 because of her childhood experience I immediately knew she was telling the truth and woman should never question her statement for the following reason:

I mentioned before that ***Abused women take precautions*** that is a foreign concept to a person that has not been involved in violence. When I have lived alone, ***I have always locked my bedroom door when I go to bed to sleep at night.*** I have always done it since I was nineteen years old but didn't know why I did it. *I* also ***always keep my front and back doors locked, even during the day and my car doors always stay locked.*** It has always frustrated my husband but he always keeps his house and car keys with him at all times so he can get in. I do it so I will feel safe but I never knew why it was so important to me, but remember your subconscious has one job, to protect you from real or imagined fears.

Someone that has been violated, raped and traumatized has lost their ability to feel safe and secure so their subconscious is constantly in protective mode.

I never knew if the baby's daddy was my first love that broke my heart or the people that raped me. All I know is that neither of them would be worthy of me or the baby.

I never found out if I was drugged by someone I worked with or a stranger. God walked in when I thought I was totally alone and took the baby to heaven & helped me heal. My first love experience and the rape made me very distrustful of men and influenced my future relationships with men.

I said Larry was my first love but he actually wasn't my first love. When I turned eighteen, I went to California to visit an Aunt and I met a sailor and after I went back home to Kansas I traveled back to San Diego and he asked me to marry him. But before we got married, I decided that we probably were not a good marriage fit so I broke it off and several months later went back to Kansas.

In the past fifty-five years I have had flashes of bits and pieces of my earlier years but it didn't fit together until I started to write about my life. Once I started writing the memories appeared on the computer screen and the tears started to flow.

I just pushed all of the pain and memories in the back of my subconscious and I thought I could forget and life would magically work out. But just because you don't talk about a problem doesn't mean it has gone away. It is still there, swelling, festering, just like a blister waiting to burst open and cause havoc on you years later. It can affect your ability to develop and build lasting relationships because you have an inability to trust and show love. In my case what made it worse was that I was unaware of the extent of my lack of ability to trust until now. It is not a unique situation to me. How are you? How is your past affecting your current relationships?

You can change it in the HERE and NOW! Don't waste time allowing your past experiences ruin your present and future. **Leave behind a Legacy Of Peace, Happiness and Love!**

CHAPTER 3

DID YOU ASK THE RIGHT QUESTIONS TO CHANGE THE OUTCOME OF YOUR LEGACY?

I don't think I have met anyone that hasn't had a few regrets and wished they could have a do-over at some point in their life.

This chapter will have a few of those stories from people that might have wanted to re-write a portion of their history, including me.

As you read maybe you will see a part of you in a story or two.

Chapter Includes:
- Life is Choice, Not Chance.
- The Life Altering Decision
- (Always Ask Questions)
- Is Your Past Defining Your Future?

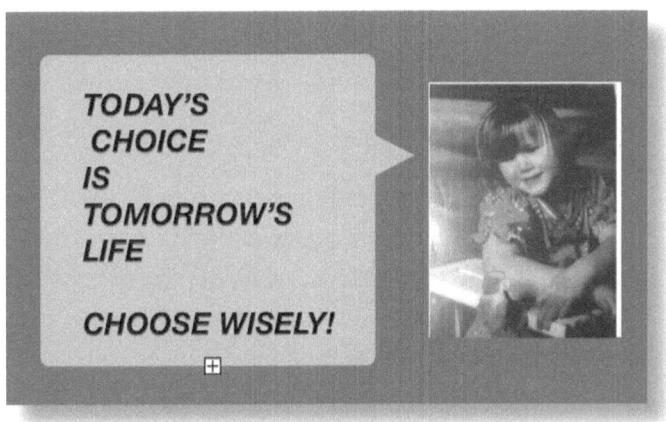

Life is Choice, Not Chance!

A couple of stories I would like to share. In 1998 I had tumors removed from my ovaries, along with my ovaries. It required two surgeons because they were attached to both my stomach and colon. Fortunately, I didn't need any additional treatment.

Last year I had tumors attached to my parathyroid glands so tumors and the parathyroid glands were removed. Everything went back to what would seem to be normal for someone that has toxic chemicals still in their body.

Approximately seven years ago one of my very good friends was diagnosed with kidney cancer. I began researching and for the next couple of months I sat down and showed her my information along with my recommendation for her to go to Huntsman Cancer Institute in Utah. The reasons I made the recommendation was because they treated the entire patient, not just the disease.

They not only recommended traditional treatment, they started you on a nutritional program, and they included hypnotherapy, meditation, acupuncture, massage therapy, osteopathic services, cooking classes, music and art therapy, tai chi/qigong, yoga and several other classes including classes that gave you a basic understanding of cancer and their approach to healing the disease, not managing it. But she didn't want to leave her family and go to Utah.

She stayed in Idaho and for one of the critical months that it would be important to work on healing the cancer everything was on hold while her doctor was on vacation, and she continued to get weaker. By the time she decided that she would like to go to Huntsman she was too weak to travel. She died approximately 3 months later.

That led me on a search to find better cancer options besides the option to destroy all of the cells including the healthy cells and hope the patient will actually survive when it's over. Since that time, I have had a number of my clients that came to me because they were diagnosed with different forms of cancer.

Each time I would help them research and I would get them in touch with cancer mentors that I had built an alliance with over the years.

Some would fly to Mexico for help and others would go to retreats in the USA. I would do conference webinars with a few clients and put them in touch with some of cancer mentors that I felt could help them. Others I would loan Videos and Books.

I had a conversation with a couple of friends about cancer and what causes it and when I said that in some cases it is possible that people can have genetic tendencies for cancer however there is a far greater degree of probability that we are susceptible to getting cancer due to Lifestyle and Environmental toxins and if we will make changes in the what we eat, the products we use and clean with we can make an enormous difference in our health.

I said that Cancer absolutely loves Sugar which is what is you can expect to get in the Standard American Diet. They both immediately said I was wrong. Lifestyle and environment had nothing to do with it. It was definitely genetics.

If someone has previously had cancer and they believe they have cancer because of genetics they won't make the lifestyle changes necessary to make sure they stay cancer-free. They do not understand that chemotherapy is not a cancer cure. It is a cancer management program. The patient needs to become an active participant if they want to be healthy.

One of my friends said she would believe that lifestyle and environment can cause cancer if I can show her documented proof and she has a valid point. I can show tons of literature but I don't do the work for my clients. I show them where to go to find the research. My question should have been:

Ask your oncologist that same question. I give my clients a list of twenty questions to ask their oncologist before he pumps that toxic chemical in their body. They need to know what they are dealing with before they say yes to something that will destroy their immune system. Good nutrition and chemical free cleaning products won't kill them.

One out of three people will get cancer in a lifetime but only two out of 100 that are diagnosed with cancer will be diagnosed due to genetics.

I have a wonderful church that my husband and I started going to a couple of years ago and I can't believe that God would put so many special people all under one roof but he did. But one thing really bothered me, there have been so many people that have been diagnosed with different forms of cancer.

After working with so many clients that have had cancer over the last several years and spending years researching such a devastating disease, I knew there had to be a better way to cure cancer than surgery, chemotherapy and radiation.

One of the first things I figured out about cancer treatment was that chemotherapy was not a cancer cure, it was a way to manage cancer. Over the years I have talked to many people that have been diagnosed with cancer. Many of them have not had the cancer return and there are many that unfortunately have had the cancer return. Some would tell me that the original Cancer was one type of cancer and if they had a reoccurrence it was a different type of cancer. When I started reading about the disease the research would say that if the cancer came back in a different location it didn't mean it was a different type of cancer. It normally would just mean that the original cancer had been dormant for a period of time in the body and it was resurfacing as the original cancer to a new location.

My question isn't: *What type of Cancer do you have?* My question is *Do you know how you got the Cancer?* You need to be able to answer that question because if you can't answer it no matter what the Doctor does, or doesn't do there is a high probable chance it will come back if you don't solve the problem that led to the situation. My next question is *What are YOU going to do about it?* Most people go to the oncologist and expect him/her to fix them and that is like playing with Russian roulette.

Through research and experience *I believe that the majority of all cancers come from two major sources: Lifestyle Choices/Environmental Toxins.* Now before I get any emails and phone calls telling me I am wrong and that you are sure you have a genetic predisposition to cancer. It is true that a very small number of individuals may have genetic characteristics that may (not will) make them more susceptible to a particular cancer but that does not mean they will get the cancer.

Does that mean they should become an active participant in their own health and cancer prevention plan? Absolutely! How do you do that? Two things I know about Cancer for sure. *Cancer hates heat and alkalinity and it loves sugar. So, give your body the two things it hates and deprive it of the one thing it loves.* Several months ago, I started praying for guidance as I was talking with several of my friends at church that had health issues, including cancer.

Since I have a "War Room" in my closet where I go and pray about everything, everyone and every problem I decided to take this problem to the war room and put it on my "war room bulletin board." Within a few days I was led to two books and I promptly went on Amazon and ordered them. The first was "Why Christians Get Cancer" and the second book was "God's Way." They were written by Rev George Malkmus who founded Hallelujah Acres in North Carolina after he was diagnosed with Cancer and healed through nutrition by following the scriptures and the teachings of the Bible. There is a statement I have said and every mentor has said for years:

"If lifestyle caused the problem, lifestyle can fix the problem!" and the beauty of it is there are no side effects. God sent me to the books and now I am forwarding his message to you. You don't have to wait until you get a chronic illness or get cancer to listen to God. The doctor doesn't have the long-term solution. You need to make lifestyle changes and I can make suggestions but you will need to do the heavy lifting. It all starts with the decision to take responsibility for you own health care decisions instead of just letting the doctor handle your disease management.

The choice is yours.
*I hope you make the right on*e.

The Life Altering Decision
(always ask questions)

I asked God for help and direction and he led me to the answers.

You can let the events of life control your life or you can take control

I was hanging out with a couple of my former beauty consultants and they had both made a decision that had fascinated me, one that if I chose to make the same decision, I would soon end up regretting and continue to regret for years to come.

One of my friends and former Mary Kay Directors worked for a plastic surgeon and she decided to get Saline Breast Implants. (The safe Ones). We went into a restaurant restroom one evening and she proudly produced her new boobs for the whole world to see. A very fine specimen indeed.

I must say they were impressive. She raved about them explaining how they had improved her social life and her charm. After she finished her breast implant speech, we were all ready to jump on the "Big Boob" band wagon. Both my other friend and I became part of the next wave of surgery recipients. At this point I should say that I had never been sick a day in my life up to this point. I had my surgery in October, 1987 and for the next three months I was extremely happy.

But in January, 1988 I started having severe bone and joint pain in my thumbs. I had no insurance so my options were somewhat limited but I went to a hand specialist and he did an X-ray. He couldn't explain the problem but he said that for some reason my thumb joint bones were bone on bone. The only thing he could do was make some braces out of plaster and suggest that I wear them, especially when I did anything that required lifting or repetitive use of my hands.

I made an appointment with my plastic surgeon and asked him if for any reason he thought that the breast implants could have caused the problem. He said "No." I really didn't expect him to say anything else. My other friend developed "Fibromyalgia" symptoms within a few months.

My friend that worked for the plastic surgeon has developed heart problems which may or may not be attributed to her implants. I have not stayed in contact with her so it is difficult for me to answer that question.

Lesson #15
When you reach an obstacle, turn it into an opportunity. You have the choice. Refuse to throw in the towel. It is far better to be exhausted from success than to be rested from failure. – Mary Kay Ash

I had met my current husband and we were about to be married. He would have been very supportive if I had decided to pick up the Mary Kay business and run with it but something happened that caused me to totally change the direction of my life.

If the hand joint problems were the only problems, I had I would have never connected it to breast implants but the story doesn't end here, it is just beginning. Less than a year later I began having neurological stroke like symptoms, including slurred speech, inability to walk and brain fog.

Even though I had a very troublesome neurological condition that caused major problems when I wasn't in remission (which was most of the time) I was very active in to community and in my business. I was President of both my sorority and Soroptimist at different times and held other offices as well. I was the public awareness chair for Habitat for Humanity so I was on television quite frequently promoting all three organizations.

I also traveled across the country taking additional continuing higher educational programs for business and my hypnotherapy practice. I never knew when I was going to have a neurological problem so Ron went to almost every meeting with me so he could help me leave through back entrances if I should have a problem. He got an award for perfect attendance the year I was President of Soroptimist. He was still working back then and had to get up at 4:00 am so it was over and above the call of husband duty but he took it in his stride.

I was also securities and insurance licensed and I was in a business for a while called WMA Securities. I happened to be at the office for a business meeting one evening when I had a neurological episode. It took two people to get me down the stairs and into the car. Ron rushed me to the hospital for tests and blood work and all of the tests they ordered came back normal but that was because they were running normal tests instead of a toxicology panel. You need to sometimes step outside of the box. If you see how serious the patient's condition is and everything is normal you start asking questions.

You don't assume everything is normal. Doctors don't like to question doctors. They assume the patient doesn't know what they are talking about. Doctors need to pay more attention to what the patient is saying. The patient will give you clues to both the ***problem*** & the ***solution.***

Learn To Count Your Blessings..... Miracles Happen...

Lesson #16
"God Does The Thinking But We Need To Do The Leg Work"....Quote by Judie Dietzler

I have been symptom free since 2011. Some people would call it a miracle. I would call it a combination of a miracle, guidance from God, and hard work on my part. I found that every time I went to my traditional physician and gave him/her a list of potential symptoms I would receive prescriptions which only added to the problem.

So I discovered that my best friend was my computer and google. I knew the problem began exactly three months after breast implants. So, I decided to research the ingredients that were in implants. I wanted to know if there was a chance that the body would try and reject an implant and if there had been any problems in the past with implants.

My research lead to hundreds of women all across the country that were very sick and doctors that were removing the implants. Hindsight is always 20/20. Wouldn't it be wonderful if I had decided to do all of this great research BEFORE I said yes to breast augmentation?

But of course, my life story and career choices would have been much shorter. The plastic surgeon that did my surgery retired immediately after the heat of the class action law suits began and women were going to his office wanting their surgery records. But he didn't need to worry. All he needed to do was wait until the heat from all of the publicity blew over and it would go back to business as usual. The sick patients would be swept under the carpet and no-one would be wiser or care. They would just slink away in pain.

Ron and I went on with our life like everyone else, after I managed to get a handle on my health situation. I was lucky to have such a wonderful man. I was still the beautiful woman he married even without implants. They weren't a deal breaker for his love. I paid $3,000 to get them and He paid $16,000 to get them removed and they are sitting on a shelf in the garage.

What did I learn from this experience?

Lesson #17
Real Beauty begins on the inside and shines through to the outside!

The physical body is such an insignificant part of the big picture and it lasts for such a short fleeting minute. We need to understand that there is more to the human anatomy than what you see visually. Why would we want to take the perfect image that God made and mold it into a re-make of the man-made perfect image. When you mess with perfection you make changes to the DNA of our body.

What I learned from my years researching breast implants & talking to experts: Always ask a lot of questions.

A few years ago, I worked with a Breast Implant Support Group and within the group the ladies had many illnesses. Some had conditions that were annoying, others had chronic problems, and many had life threatening conditions. Each had turned to the traditional medical community for help to no avail. Blood tests, Cat Scans, MRI, XRAY's Pet Scans plus so much more were done but according to the doctors the tests were normal. But the women were anything but normal.

These were ladies that were in excellent health before they decided to get breast implants. The only reason they got breast implants was they thought the implants would enhance their appearance and self-image. Each of them said that if they were told that there was the slightest chance, they would be trading their health for an enhanced self-image not one of them would have chosen implants, including me. I lost my career because of that spur of the moment choice and following the crowd instead of listening to my wiser "inner voice."

I shared my story. Healthy, I never got so much as a cold. I had the safe saline breast implants October, 1987 and three months later I started having pain in both hands followed by neurological stroke like symptoms less than a year later.

All of the tests would come back normal but later on I discovered that the reason every test was normal was because they didn't do the right type of test. A seminar was held in Boise, Idaho and doctors were brought in that understood what happens with both silicone and saline implants when they are implanted in the human body.

After attending the seminar, I understood completely why my body was reacting the way it was and if I was going to have any chance of regaining my health, I needed to remove the implants. I knew I couldn't have a doctor in my home state remove them because in order to fix a problem you have to first admit there is a problem and I didn't know of any doctors that I trusted to safely remove the implants. You not only needed to remove the implant but you need to remove the shell.

But one of the seminar speakers, Dr. Wood, was a plastic surgeon from California and he had removed many implants and did reconstruction using the patient's own breast tissue so I made an appointment to go see him. When my implants were removed mold was found surrounding both implant nipples and severe vasculitis on the chest wall of each breast.

It is wonderful to be married to a man that loves you no matter what. I told him about the implants and that I didn't know if removing them would make me better but I said my greatest fear was that if I didn't remove them my health would get much worse.

I told him about some of the women I met at the seminar. Some walked in, some were on crutches, others in wheel chairs. Others couldn't come because they were too sick but they all had two things in common:

1. They all had breast implants.
2. They were all between the ages of 18-40.

We flew to California in 1990 so I could have surgery to remove my breast implants. I had severe vasculitis in both breasts and one of the implants had a slow leak. In addition, there was mold around the nipple area of both breasts. I had breast implants a little over two years.

From all of the research and doctors I have talked to over the years there are two things that I feel with certainty:

1. All Breast implants will leak or rupture
2. If you have them it won't be your last surgery (It is recommended you replace them every 10 years) If you are not replacing them as recommended you are playing Russian roulette with your health.

I would like to say that I was magically cured but that didn't happen. What did happen was I continued to research and stay away from traditional doctors as much as possible. I discovered that many of the medication I was being prescribed would either interfere with my migraine medication or it would cause the stroke-like symptoms because the medications had similar chemicals as the toxic chemicals that were already causing problems in my body. I did much better if I went to Naturopathic or Osteopathic Physicians.

I found that certain smells and products would trigger the symptoms so in 2000 I decided to remove all of the toxic chemicals from my life, at least as much as possible. I boxed all of my body care, hair care, skin care, cosmetics, cleaning products, laundry detergent, etc. and put them by the curb for the sanitation department to take to the dump. They put a big yellow tag on the box that said "Hazardous Waste" dispose of yourself. The products I was using was too hazardous for the dump but I was using them on my body and in my home every day. That was when I knew I might be on the right path. I now order everything from an Idaho Company that has Chemical Free Products. I have been symptom free since 2011. (since switching to Melaleuca's toxic free products).

Of course, in church you may occasionally see me move to a different location if I am sitting behind someone that has lathered on the toxic over-the-counter perfume. I should clarify "symptom free." I am not having neurological symptoms, which was the most devastating of my symptoms. I still have the severe pain in my thumbs and they have wanted to do surgery on my thumbs for at least twenty years but I have resisted. I wrote a book on toxic chemicals in 2016 called "Your Toxic Enemy, How to Heal and Thrive in A Toxic World" and before I wrote the book I flew to Atlanta, Georgia to talk to Dr. Susan Kolb at Plastikos Plastic Surgery.

Many of her patients were there to have implants removed and learn ways to improve their health. She tested me and I finally had a better understanding of my health. She said that I definitely had neurotoxicity and also mold in the eye socket. Knowing that didn't fix either problem because I came back to Idaho where I still couldn't find a doctor that would admit breast implants could cause a problem and since they couldn't understand how there could possibly be a problem, they also didn't have a solution.

A couple of problems that all breast implant recipient women seem to have in common is sleep disturbance, vision problems, bone and joint problems, brain fog, sinus problems, and other non-specific problems.

I have been on a sleep aid for approximately twenty years, I have had para thyroid tumors removed, tumors on both ovaries removed along with the ovaries, pain in all of my joints, all of these problems began after made a decision to get breast implants.

Do you know that most people don't get cancer because that have bad genes? There are two main reasons, lifestyle and environmental toxins. But I am certainly not the only person that has suffered because of "safe breast implants:

One of the support group members was a young vibrant mother of two small children who was healthy and had never been sick. She thought she had asked her plastic surgeon all of the right questions. Her doctor told her the implants would go with her to the grave, *(did he mean in your 30's or 90's?).*

She asked if anyone had ever had them taken out and he said yes but only because they didn't like them. He never told her that she was risking messing up her central nervous system or that she would develop severe brain fog. He didn't discuss the seriousness of autoimmune diseases or the fact that they are incurable. She got saline implants and within eight months she had symptoms so severe she couldn't function or take care of her kids. She couldn't retain anything she read, always tired, sleep disturbances, heart palpitations, hands tingling, autoimmune problems.

She was one of the lucky ladies. Approximately two years after she had her implants removed, she is back to normal and has regained most of her health back, at least for now. Not everyone that gets breast implants are that fortunate.

Another Support group member had saline implants and like most women she was told they would last a lifetime. She suffered for nine years with pain, brain fog and constantly being tired but it never occurred to her that her implants could be causing the problem until she finally made the decision to have them removed. She started to see an improvement and now, two years later she feels so much better. She made this statement: "The longer you have them the sicker you can get. You need to make the decision to do what is best to heal your body."

Another lady in the group went out of state to a doctor to find out why she was so sick only to discover that her problem was also Silicone sickness from the saline silicone shell but the entire shell was covered in mold. She was experiencing weight gain, vision loss and burning pain. She said she had been to so many doctors with no answers that she thought she was going to die before she got any answers. I escorted her to California so she could have testing and she also had the implants removed.

She loved them and they looked great, up until the day she took them out. But a couple of years ago she started having gallbladder problems and her lymph nodes became blocked along with digestive problems, food sensitivities and chronic infections. Then she ran into a friend that was part of the implant support group and she told her she had just had her implants removed because she had been having the same type of symptoms.

After careful consideration she decided to remove her implants. She knew that there were no guarantees that removing them would improve her symptoms but since she had been symptom-free before the implants she felt she had a better chance of healing without the implants. It has been five years since she had the implants removed and she isn't completely free of symptoms but she is so much better and she feels that she is glad she made the decision to remove them.

If you need a doctor you can go to: **www.HolisticMedicine.org**

One last story I would like to share. I met someone that has had breast implants for approximately thirty years. That is a very long time to have the same set of implants. It is so hard for me to imagine any implant lasting that long. For a number of years, she has had a severe cough in the morning but it usually improves later in the day. I did background research and I believe it is the silicone shell that is separating and going to different parts of her body, primarily her lungs. To verify the research, I contacted a doctor that I talked to when I wrote my last book and she said it is very common for the shell to disintegrate with age and a cough is a common symptom.

Manufacturers of implants recommend replacing implants EVERY TEN YEARS as a health and safety precaution.

I just completed some additional research and I ran across an article from the doctor that tested me and she has a list of the major symptoms of Silicone Toxicity and listed among them is Throat Clearing, Cough and Difficult Swallowing. She states in the article that if you have any of the symptoms listed below you need to have the implants removed as soon as possible.

We don't always listen to good advice. I know I haven't always listened to the good advice I've been given. Sometimes we have to learn the hard way. I remember how hard it was for me to make the decision to remove my implants but when the choice was whether to live or potentially die, the choice was much easier to make.

It was much easier knowing I had a very loving supportive partner that wanted the very best for me and he would love me even if my tits were on my back. If you have implants and you get mammograms, it will put a huge strain on breast implants. In the first place it is much harder to detect cancer with a mammogram when you have breast implants. I always recommend thermograms for two reasons: 1. It is easier to detect the cancer cells with a thermogram and (2) Protecting your implants from a potential rupture.

"The Wheel That Squeaks the Loudest Is the One That Gets Heard"

That is exactly what happened! Women were sick, they felt they had been deceived and they were mad. When I had my implants removed in 2000 there was so much pressure put on the manufacturers of breast implants that women weren't getting silicone implants and there were hundreds of class action lawsuits against breast implant manufacturers because women were getting sick and many were dying.

From what I can tell from the women I have talked to and from my own personal experience, we haven't received a dime in compensation from any class action law suit, we have spent a fortune in medical bills over the years, we still have health challenges, the companies are back to selling both silicone and saline implants, and the plastic surgeons are making a fortune providing the new "breast implants" without sharing a complete picture of any of the "Risks of having Breast Implants."

Breast Implant Risks:

- infection (bacteria and mold which can be released from the implant into the body).
- surgical Risks
- anesthesia risks
- chronic breast pain,
- breast or nipple numbness
- capsular contracture
- scar tissue
- hardened and misshapen breasts
- breakage and leakage
- necrosis (skin death)
- dissatisfaction with how the breast looks
- disfigurement
- arthritis and joint pain
- fatigue
- need for additional surgery to deal with problem
- memory loss
- cognitive impairment: poor concentration
- metal poisoning due to platinum exposure (in silicone implants)
- silicone migration into lymph nodes and other organs
- debilitating autoimmune disease such as fibromyalgia, dermatomyositis,
- polymyositis, Hashimoto's thyroiditis, mixed connective-tissue disease, pulmonary
- fibrosis, eosinophilic fasciitis, and polymyalgia.
- And last but not least, death (after all it was only a women's issue) and it was back to business as usual.

- There is no such thing as a safe breast implant. Not only are they not life-saving and totally unnecessary, they are dangerous to health and well-being. If you need just a little more knowledge before jumping into the deep end here is one final bit of information that I will share if you currently have breast implants and are experiencing symptoms.

SYMPTOMS OF SILICONE TOXICITY:
Breast implant illness is a period of sickness affecting the body caused by silicone or saline breast implants.

According to plastic surgeon Dr. Susan Kolb "it is my personal opinion that if you are experiencing the symptoms below, it is your body indicating to you that the implants are causing illness and should be removed as soon as possible."

- FATIGUE OR CHRONIC FATIGUE
- COGNITIVE DYSFUNCTION (BRAIN FOG, DIFFICULTY CONCENTRATING, MUSCLE PAIN AND WEAKNESS, JOINT PAIN
- HAIR LOSS, DRY SKIN AND HAIR
- DRY EYES, DECLINE IN VISION, VISION DISTURBANCES
- HYPO/HYPER THYROID SYMPTOMS
- HYPO/HYPER ADRENAL SYMPTOMS
- ESTROGEN/PROGESTERONE IMBALANCE OR DIMINISHING HORMONES
- HYSTERECTOMY
- THROAT CLEARING, COUGH, DIFFICULTY SWALLOWING, CHOKING, REFLUX, METALLIC TASTES
- LOW LIBIDO
- SLOW HEALING OF CUTS AND SCRAPES, EASY BRUISING
- MEMORY LOSS)
- REFLUX, METALLIC TASTES
- POOR SLEEP AND INSOMNIA VERTIGO
- WEIGHT PROBLEMS
- INFLAMMATION

- PREMATURE AGING
- PANCREATITIS
- GASTROINTESTINAL AND DIGESTIVE ISSUES SUCH AS IBS, ACID REFLUX, GERD, GASTRITIS
- FEVERS, NIGHT SWEATS, INTOLERANT TO HEAT/COLD
- NEW AND PERSISTENT BACTERIAL AND VIRAL INFECTIONS
- SLOW CLEARING OF COMMON COLDS AND FLUES

I remember how excited all of my friends and I were years ago when we made the decision to improve our self-image and add breast implants as if we were choosing a new shade of lipstick. Not aware of what was in store for us in the future. We had no idea that our decision had the potential to shorten our life. This part of my life story has been so difficult for me to write because I have spent years not letting a soul know the source of my toxic contamination but I couldn't share the story of my life, my thoughts, without sharing this part of my life, even though it was a very painful part.

What is so sad is that not everyone that decides on breast implants makes that choice just because of self-image alone. They do it because they are a cancer survivor and they had a mastectomy. Sometimes women feel that in order to be a whole woman they need to look a certain way and anything less than two breasts won't make them complete. We need to rethink and re-educate about self-image. There are other ways to enhance the breast if that is really that important by using actual tissue from other areas of the body.

I am not an expert on the subject but check with a plastic surgeon about Tissue Flap Surgery called autologous tissue reconstruction. All breast implants impair our immune system and the silicone shell deteriorates, releasing toxins, allowing colonization and the filling whether cohesive gel, saline or gel silicone permeates the shell contaminating our body. According to several studies, most implants deteriorate and or rupture within 6 to 8 years but sooner in many cases.

Your future heath depends on making the right choice so do your research **before deciding on breast implants**. It is not an easy decision to reverse and the decision you make will **affect your health for the rest of your life.**

Adverse Breast Implant Symptoms:

Rashes, itching, skin crawling or skin irritation.
Memory loss, brain fog, forgetful, trouble concentrating, fatigue, joint, muscle pain
Random swelling autoimmune symptoms, vision changes (blurry eyes, dry eyes, watery eyes, itchy or irritated.)
Hot flashes or ice-cold body temperature
Flu or cold like symptoms, dry hair, nail, skin, eyes.
Sinus congestion or infection symptoms, trouble swallowing rashes constant need to clear throat, Raynaud's symptoms, Fibromyalgia symptoms, IBS, premature aging, headaches, dry brittle hair, trouble balancing, trouble breathing, breast pain, sensitivity, heart palpitations, chronic fatigue, insomnia, chest pain (throbbing, burning, aching,).
confusion
muscle weakness, easily bruising enlarged lymph nodes, numbness and/or tingling in body or extremities recurring yeast or UTI infections, mixing up words
sudden food/beverage sensitivities, metallic taste in mouth & more

Risks of Breast Implants on Your Body:

1. 4 Times more likely to commit suicide
2. Lowered self-esteem,
3. Breast Pain or hardness,
4. Back & Shoulder Pain, Sensitivity,
5. Implant Rupture, Hardness
6. Joint Pain & other Autoimmune Symptoms
7. Fatigue
8. ALCL a type of Cancer

I ran across a poem written by a breast implant survivor named Dana Christine Schmidt. She also made the decision to get saline breast implants at the same age I decided to make that fate-full decision.

Her symptoms started within two months after she had the surgery. My symptoms began within three months after surgery.

Here is her story:
Past Is First, Futures Last, In The End We Begin

I'm feeling tired and alone, I am barely hanging on....

My body screams out in pains, while Illness takes me away...

My heart's been crushed and shattered more, than I had ever imagined before. Help me please this I ask, the strength I need is in your grasp...

I have held on for so very long, I made a mistake. Yes I was wrong. to suffer years as I have, I feel so very lost and sad...

I believed back then that I would live, now I exist and hope to give. My truths I tell for all who hear, to save them from many painful years...

As I swell, I refuse to dwell, what could have been, way back when. I share with all, because I care...

Please listen to all who have lived to say, don't let implants steal your life away. Lies have been told then and now, by greedy ones the law allows...

Out of reach to feed the greed, so many of us in desperate need. The price to save our very lives, leaves us planning our goodbyes...

Go to the website below for more breast implant info:
http://www.theunbrokensmile.com/breast-implant-illness-poem/

Dedicated to all Ladies suffering from "BII"
(C) Dana Christine Schmidt

Is Your Past Defining Your Future?

My Broken Family Does Not Define Me. Most adults remember the majority of their childhood but that isn't the case with me. I only remember small portions from birth to age twelve and even only sporadic memories of my mid-teens.

I was hesitant to include it in the book but it is difficult to write a life story and not put your entire life in the book.

What I didn't expect to happen as I began to write the book was to have memories start pouring onto the pages. The more I typed, the more I began to cry and the pent-up emotions I had held so close to my heart for so long came to the surface.

For this reason alone, I recommend that everyone keeps a journal or writes their life story so they can pass it along to their family or if for no other reason they can release any painful emotions they may have locked away in the recesses of their mind.

You may not have a trauma that you need to deal with but there may be unresolved issues from your past that are affecting the way you are handling situations in your life today.

I remember some of my abuse but it was hazy, other things that happened had been totally blocked out until fifty-five years later when I began writing on the pages of this book.

But what happened from the age of birth to nineteen helped create the environment for several engagements and break-ups, hot-headed temper tantrums when I was younger, three marriages and two divorces.

My life didn't start out stable because my Mother and Dad got divorced when I was a baby and I spent the first two years of my life living with my grandparents on a farm so my mother could live out her dream as a trapeze star in a circus.

That career ended as soon as a grizzly bear discovered Mother standing in the entrance wearing a fur coat that resembled one of her grizzly friends and attempted to maul her to death. A sailor jumped over the rail and pulled the furry beast off of her and saved her but it ended her career.

So, she then found my next daddy and refused to let my real daddy come near me.

I had been sexually abused for a long time by my step-dad, but I never blamed him because I remember that when I was sick, he would stay home from work and take care of me, not my mother. I also remember that in the winter when there was snow on the ground he would go outside and help me build a snow fort and have snowball fights with me.

When I started dating, he was the one that waited up until I got home and if he didn't think I got out of the car quick enough he would flip the porch light on and off to let me know it was time to come inside. I don't remember when the abuse began but my mother knew about it and chose to do nothing about it. I discovered he wasn't my real dad when I was sixteen and not too long after finding out I decided to leave home. My cousin and I moved into an apartment together and she quit school but I decided to stay in school during the day and work at a drive-in theater at night so I could pay my rent.

My childhood was so bad and yet I have never been cruel or mean to my parents. My siblings, mother and I were on our way to Fredonia, Kansas a number of years ago when my mother suddenly blurted out "I had to watch my husband molest my daughter over and over again." I temporarily stopped breathing. That was the first time I knew that my mother was aware I had been sexually abused. There was dead silence in the car for the rest of the trip. When we got back to Wichita, Kansas I cornered my mother in the kitchen and asked her if she knew why didn't she ever say anything? She said, "If she said something, she would have to do something and she wasn't prepared to do something because she had three (at the time) small children and no training to take care of them financially. I never brought it up again. My step-dad died when he was forty-five and the kids were still very young.

My brother and sisters wore the most expensive clothes to church but they only had one outfit because when you buy the best and you don't have much money, you can't afford much. My mom didn't teach them any values to live by because she didn't learn values from her parents. My brother developed a much higher personal and professional value system than he could have ever learned from our mother.

Lesson #18
Don't worry that you can't give your kids the best of everything. Give them your very best!

- I really got lucky when God sent me my brother.

- We came from such a crazy mixed up family but he has always been there for me.

- Not many siblings would kidnap someone for you but he didn't hesitate.

- When my granddaughter died, he was immediately on my door step.

- When I was in surgery and they were getting ready to operate on me, they suddenly brought a phone to me and it was my brother letting me know he was praying for me.

- How blessed I am to call Howard my brother. You can pick your friends but you can't pick your family.

Thank you, God, for giving me a wonderful brother.

Lesson #19
It's not what happens to you in life that's important, it's how you interpret what happens to you in life …..quote by Judie Dietzler

Sometimes a family will have children and only give them basic needs: Food, shelter, clothes and they grow up get a job and retire without discovering their true God given gifts. They die thinking their only value was the dollar amount of a monthly paycheck or social security check with their music inside them still unplayed.

If their only legacy is a social security check it will vanish when they take their last breath. A legacy is something you can leave behind that will say your life will have value to humanity long after you are gone.

If this book will help one person in the future know that they do not have to be a victim of abuse, they can survive and thrive, then it will be worth the heartache of reliving the pain.

We are influenced by our environment and the environment I was raised in was not loving by any stretch of the imagination. I didn't see loving relationships so I didn't learn how to build or develop a relationship. I learned by trial and error. I had never been exposed to healthy relationships, male or female until I was part of Mary Kay Cosmetics. I just realized this the moment I started writing this paragraph. How sad. I now know how to walk away from toxic relationships.

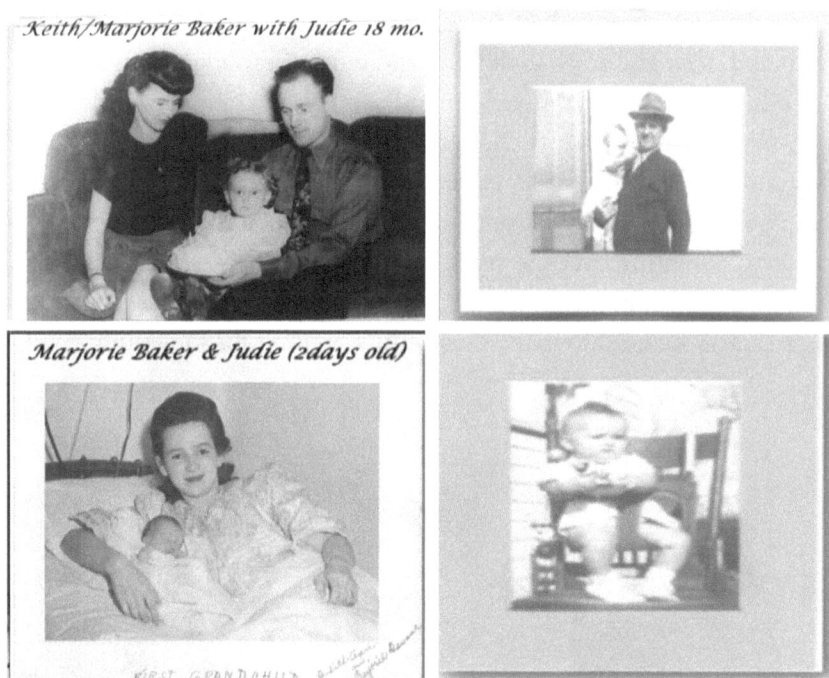

Lesson #20
Make Peace with The Past So You Won't Mess Up the Present

My step-dad died when he was forty-five and the kids were still very young. They went to church on Sunday but never Sunday school so the kids didn't have an opportunity to learn any bible stories. My mother went to church so she could admire everyone's clothes and show off her clothes. I know I didn't ever get my mother's time and it was probably the same with my siblings. You just couldn't have an in-depth conversation with her. You could only have surface conversations that didn't require her to think.

You can pick your friends but you can't pick your family..........

Sometimes our kids might feel like a revised version of "musical Chairs" called "Musical Families". Families should find a better solution I now went from one dad to a new dad & my mother didn't want my birth dad to be part of my life for the rest of my life, so his name was never mentioned.

It has taken me almost a half century to understand the trauma from my childhood, teen and early adult years and most of my adult years to brush the dust from my crazy, mixed-up and sometimes traumatic childhood. My parents made the worst choices a parent could ever make with all of their children and they never learned any parenting skills. My Mother is Ninety-Three and I would love to say she has learned the meaning of love and good parenting over the years but I am sure that isn't the case. The past is no longer important to me. I believe we only have so much time here on earth and we need to make those minutes count for something good.

CHAPTER 4

LEGACY OF LOVE

This chapter represents the men that were my husbands and the first love that I was engage to when I was nineteen years old.

What is Love?

>Love is patient and kind;
>Love does not envy or boast;
>It is not arrogant or rude.
>It does not insist on its own way; it is not irritable or resentful;
>It does not rejoice at wrongdoing, but rejoices with the truth.
>Love bears all things
>Believes all things
>Hopes all things,
>Endures all things.

Chapter Includes:

- First Marriage-Dave Schmidt
- Second Marriage-Jim Burns
- Third Marriage-Ron Dietzler
- What are the lessons I learned from my marriages?
- First Love-Larry Huckleberry

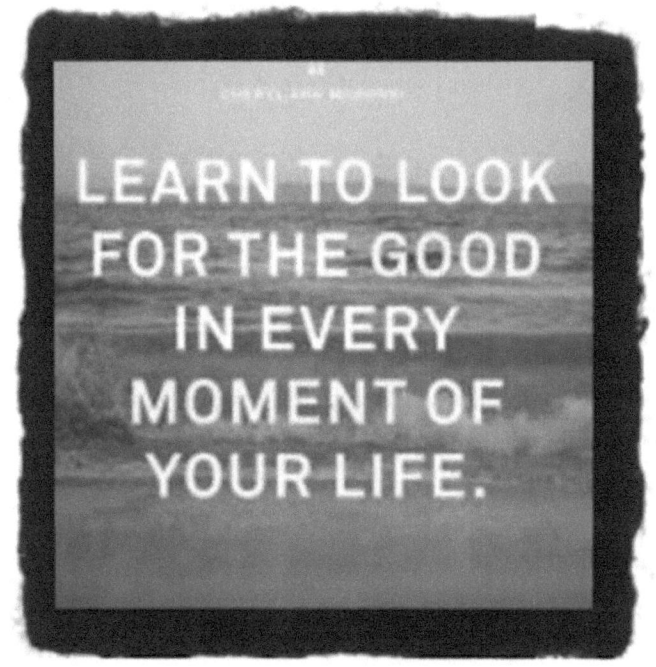

Lessons from Marriage - part 1
Can you turn back the clock?

My Place in this world: Wife, mother, family
I met Dave in a Kings X Drive inn restaurant one evening after working the evening shift at Wesley Medical Center in Wichita, Kansas. He was easy going and a lot of fun.

We got married about six months after we met. Our first home had one time been an army barracks. We painted and attempted to wallpaper it. In the middle of the night one night we heard a sound like, snap, crackle, pop. We got up and turned the light on to discover our wallpaper was falling off the wall. (tip: never wallpaper on a wall that doesn't have a smooth surface)

I took marriage serious and since I had never learned to cook except snickerdoodles in home economics class in school, I had a learning curve going for me. The good news was that my husband was easy going and he would eat anything I fixed and praise me for it, thank heaven. If that wasn't the case, I would have burst out into tears I am sure.

I loved being in this huge family, and what was even better was they all seemed to like each other. That was unheard of in my family. Everyone got together for Thanksgiving and Christmas. Thanksgiving was usually at Bill and Lucille Phillips house because they had the space for everyone. After Dinner everyone would sit around and play games and snack before going home.

After all these years I still remember and miss those get togethers. Lucille was a great artist and she painted a beautiful piece of artwork that I kept until just a few years ago when I gave it to my son so he would have something to remember both his dad and me in the coming years. I hope he takes care of it because it has traveled many miles and there are so many memories attached to that artwork.

We had been married almost two years when the road crew decided to resurface the roads with black tar and it was still fresh. Not realizing there was a problem I drove through the tar and immediately knew there was a problem when I saw black tar sticking to our new white car.

I instantly panicked and the first place I decided to run and hide hoping to fix the problem was my in-laws house. We worked to try and remove it. After a few hours of not going home my husband called his dad because he was worried since I hadn't come home. His dad reassured him that I was safe and told him what had happened.

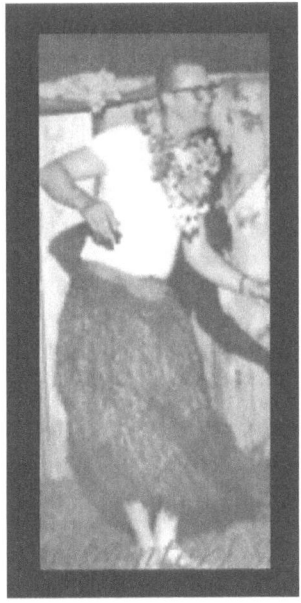

He asked to talk to me. When I got on the phone he said "Don't ever stay away because of a car. A car can be replaced. You can't. I was worried something happened to you."

I was so excited because I had joined a sorority of great new girlfriends and we bought a house in a nice neighborhood. I loved it that Dave worked for IBM and I enjoyed my job as the State Service Manager for JC Penney's. But things don't usually stay status quo. Something exciting happened. I was pregnant so 6 months later I quit my job.

My mother kept calling and wanting me to do things for her and if I said no she would wait until later and call back when Dave would answer and ask him. He was so easy going and after all she was my Mother, so he would say YES, which always locked my jaw. We had a beautiful baby boy but it was a difficult delivery and after we got home, I was now a stay at home Mom with no income so guess what came next? You guessed it! A BUDGET.

I hated a budged along with constant harassment from my mother. I wasn't sure how to budget groceries. That was totally a foreign concept to me. My sorority sisters always dressed so nice and I felt I needed to keep up with their style. I joined a gym to try and get back in shape from having a baby. Dave was really hard working and a smart computer expert so it really shocked me when he decided he was going to quit and start selling insurance.

I couldn't understand why he would want to give up the security of a great job in computers for a job that would require him to work both day and night for a very long time in order to build the business, especially since he had a small baby at home. One of the things that had attracted me to him besides his good looks, was that he was so easy going and stable and secure. He wasn't going to be a flighty job hopper.

There was so much for me to mentally digest all at one time, my mother, no longer working and earning an income, being a new mother myself, my husband catering to my mother's whims whenever she called, the budget. Everything just kept getting bigger until the molehill became a mountain and I did what seemed like the easiest solution at the time. SO I DECIDED TO SEE IF THE GRASS IS GREENER ON THE OTHER SIDE OF THE PASTURE.

I asked Dave for a divorce and needless to say he didn't take it well. We stayed under the same roof for a few months but that didn't work very well. One night I walked into the living room and he was holding our son on his lap in a chair but under the chair was a gun. I didn't even know he had a gun.

I didn't know why he had the gun or what his intentions were. If he just wanted to scare me it was working. I did the only thing I knew to do at the time, I ignored it. I thought if I made a big deal of it, things might escalate and I didn't want anything to happen to our son so I decided to do nothing and hope he would rethink whatever was going through his mind. It must have worked because by morning I didn't see any signs of the gun and he never mentioned it and I never brought it up.

I was getting ready for bed when Dave decided he wanted to discuss our divorce. I wanted to wait until the next day to talk about it but he didn't. He started arguing with me and I turned to walk away when he suddenly grabbed my throat and that was the last thing I remembered.

A few minutes later I woke up on the floor and he was standing over me. He said he was scared because he thought he had killed me. The next day he moved out until the house was sold. We decided that if he stayed, he was afraid something would happen that he would regret. Dave and I tried to live together for a while after we divorced and when he left while I was at work one day, he took everything from our past with him.

I don't know if he seriously wanted to try and work things out or if he wanted to do it long enough so he could steal our memories but when he left, he took my wedding rings, every picture of our family and Dave & me during our entire five-year marriage. Any signs that we had ever been married were gone. The only thing he left behind were two wedding pictures.

Dave had never wanted the divorce and he was devastated when we got divorced. Once the wheels were in motion, I didn't know how to reverse it and if we did get back together, I felt the problems would still be there.

I would still have the same mother. I didn't see a way out and I didn't have anyone I felt I could trust and confide in that could give me guidance. Once I started things in motion it became a run-away train that I didn't know how to stop.

Not long after we were divorced, I had to have a hysterectomy. My aunt came to the hospital and said that if Dave would come to see me she believed it would be a turning point in helping us get back together. That was unusual. My aunt didn't often offer sound advice. Dave never came to the hospital nor did we ever talk after my surgery.

The only two pictures My First Love (Dave) left.
He took or destroyed the rest.

Beautiful White 1968 Chevrolet
Camaro that I drove through Black Tar

Job I had at Wesley Medical Center
In Wichita, Kansas When I Met Dave

When I was married to Dave, I was very quiet and shy and I wasn't assertive. That was one of the reasons Dave signed me up for a Dale Carnegie Course.

One spring day he came to town from Louisiana, where he was living, and asked spend the day with his son. I said I would be working until 6:00 pm so it would be fine as long as he brought him home in time for dinner. He said no problem. I arrived home and not only my son wasn't there but Dave had broken into my house and stole all of my sons' clothes and also took his five newborn puppies.

He called a couple of hours later to tell me he had Tyson and that he was safe. I Immediately gave the phone to the police, who I had called and were at my house. He was surprised that I had called the police and what was an even bigger surprise and out of character was that I spent the next year trailing his every move, sending letters, making calls, not letting up.

He thought that once he had our son, I would let it go and not do anything but he didn't realize I had changed from the time we were married. I was no longer a little quiet mouse.

I was a mother and I was determined to not stop until I either had my son or had a sign from God that he didn't want me to have my son. Until that happened, I was going to chase him and trail his every move, even if it took my last breath.

My son, Tyson, and me in the hospital

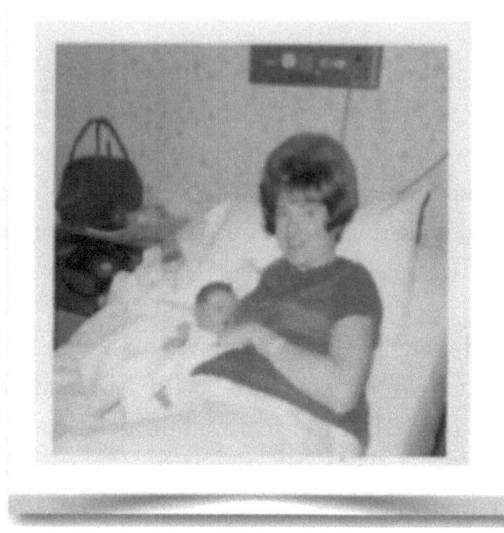

My son, Tyson with his grandparents

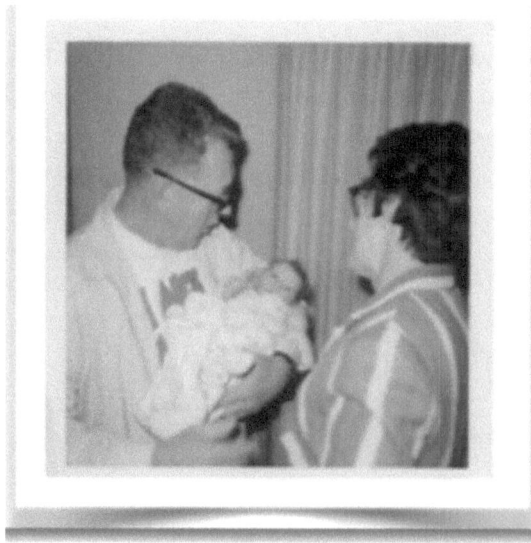

Lessons from Marriage - part 2
My Second Love Jim Burns

Lesson #21
A Successful Marriage Depends On Two Things: Finding The Right Person & Being The Right Person

After my divorce the government helped me buy a house on a 235 Government Loan and I went back to School and became a Medical Technologist working for a Doctor.

In walked Jim Burns who was handsome, outgoing, appeared to be slightly arrogant and he was one of the doctor's patients. We were both also alcoholism counselors with one exception. Jim was also a recovering alcoholic.

He had been sober for a couple of years when I met him but once you are an alcoholic you are always an alcoholic. We didn't know each other very long before we made the decision to get married. My son was still missing and after Dave discovered the police were after him, he left everything he owned and took our son and his live-in girlfriend (old enough to be his mother) and went into hiding.

I immediately began a letter writing campaign to anyone and everyone in the town he lived in previously, the friends he may or may not have, the schools they might have enrolled Tyson, and any and all police departments in surrounding states. I gave them proof that I had custody, I sent pictures and descriptions and I prayed to God for help.

In another chapter I described what it was like when we got the call to pick Tyson up.

I needed a career that I could be home but I also needed a career that I had the potential to earn a good income. If Mary Kay had come along when I was married to my first husband, I don't think I would have been motivated to do what I needed to do to be successful.

Jim wasn't anxious to look for a job but he was handy to have around the house. He drove me to my appointments and he did the monthly recognition newsletter. I would talk to him about team building and promotional ideas.

We got a training center in a mall and organized my Directors and their husbands to help build the rooms so we could hold weekly meetings and monthly team events.

Our team became a Cadillac unit in approximately three short years and I was on my way to Future National Sales Director with Mary Kay Cosmetics.

I often had to keep a tight rein on Jim and his mouth with my consultant's husband's however because he had a tendency to gossip about my consultants to other consultants' husbands, which was something I absolutely didn't allow among consultants, and it was worse to hear trash talk about the ladies from my husband. I told him if he didn't stop gossiping about my consultants he would have to stay away from sales meetings.

I had several shares of Mary Kay stock. I gave them to A G Edwards to hold for me and I called my stock broker after my divorce from Jim to see about cashing out my Mary Kay stock. *Can you imagine my surprise when I discover that A G Edwards and my stock broker allowed my EX-HUSBAND to cash out my Mary Kay Cosmetics Stock shares without getting my permission?*

(They took him at his word and gave him the money on stock shares that were not in his name.)

Neither the company nor my stock broker called to see if it was ok to cash out the stock and give the money to my ex-husband.

Sounds like Jim, my stock broker, nor the brokerage firm had integrity.

Legacy of Love
My third & Last Love - Ron Dietzler

Lesson #22
A Successful Marriage Depends on Two Things: Finding the Right Person & Being the Right Person

After all of my ups and downs and the troubles with the IRS I was both emotionally and financially drained. I still had Mary Kay customers but didn't have the desire to recruit or hold sales meetings because I had divorced my amen cheering section and my life was adrift. I had a son that was sneaking out at night hanging out with the wrong kind of people. He would hot wire my car after I went to bed at night and drive it up to the end of 8th street and do whatever you're not supposed to do.

My mechanic showed me how to take the spark plugs out of the car so he couldn't drive the car. It was costing me a fortune in repair costs because he was getting dirt in my carburetor. For some reason this kid wasn't thinking about anyone but himself. He signed up for the navy and was gone for about a year and suddenly returned home. The only explanation I could get out of him was that the Navy and him decided mutually that it was to both of their interest for him to leave the Navy.

Since when does the Navy let you just walk away. He drove his Datsun 280z to the Norfolk, Virginia Naval Base but it wasn't running when he left to come home so he came home without it. One of my truck driver friends brought the car back on one of his long-haul trips from the east coast.

Jim, who wasn't doing me any favors, helped hook my son up with a girl that wasn't a Christian or didn't have an interest in goals or staying in school.

He enrolled in a technical school and in order to help him out I purchased a six-unit apartment complex and told him he could live in one of the units rent-free as long as he was in school but if he dropped out of school, he would need to pay rent or move. I put in new carpet in his unit before he moved in and painted it. Six months later he quit the technical school and the only thing he was doing was sleeping all day, not working and not paying rent.

I had to ask him to move out. He had never been very good at cleaning or taking care of anything he had ever been given so I don't know why it surprised me when he left my apartment in a shamble. I had to go in and re-paint it and put in new carpet again after only six months. That was probably one of my greatest disappointments in my son. Destroying his stuff was one thing but to deliberately destroy something that cost me a lot of money without any remorse was something I never could understand.

His girlfriend got pregnant twice and after about five years they decided to get married but since they didn't have two nickels to rub together, they lived in his mother-in-law's garage.

I was still servicing my Mary Kay customers but in addition I started a Fundraising company and traveled half of Idaho and half of Oregon working with Elementary through High Schools. Ron and I were dating and he bought me a car because he wanted me to be safe on the roads I was traveling. He literally became indispensable to me over the next few months by taking care of my house, babysitting with my new baby puppies, and mowing my lawn. I finally decided if I didn't snatch him up someone else probably would. I told him that I was not Betty Crocker and I didn't want to spend all of my time in the kitchen. He promptly wrote on a napkin that he would take me out to eat every day if that is what I wanted.

I kept the napkin in case I needed to remind him of his words in the coming years. We got married in a little chapel called "Sweetheart Manor" surrounded by friends and a few relatives. Then off to Hawaii for our Honeymoon. By the way the hook he used to get me to marry him was ***"marry me and fly free."*** He worked for United Airlines so he thought that was a great way to get me to say YES but he forgot the rest of the story.

When you marry an airline employee you fly standby so you may not be sitting together on the plane, and even worse, you may not be on the same plane. When you leave Las Vegas, they have planes departing ever thirty minutes and we were in the airport an entire night, (24 hours), trying to come home. People gambled and lost all of their money and immediately ran to the airport to get on an earlier flight, which bumped us off the flight. We had been married less than three months when his twenty-year-old son called and said he was coming home from Park City, Utah. His Dad said "Make sure you have a place to stay, money, a job and transportation."

He came back without all four, pitched a tent in the back yard of our very small house at the time, and made no attempt to look for a job. I came home from a fundraising trip to find a Subaru Brat parked in front of our house. I walked in tired from the trip and casually asked "Who's car?" His son pipes up with a big grin on his face, "That's my car." So, I immediately said that's great. That must mean you found a good job. Right? He said No! I immediately turned to his dad and said "How could he get a car if he doesn't have a job? He can't make car payments.

His dad said. "He said he can't look for a job without a car so I co-signed for it." I said, "If he doesn't make the payments you are responsible to make the payments. Has he always been reliable in the past?" His dad said "No"

I said the car is going back and we took it back but Larry Miller Subaru wouldn't take it back. It had only been one day but according to their company we had to trade it for a different Subaru.

He then decided to join the Navy which I was proud of him for taking a step that could lead to future benefits. He does exceptionally well in a structured environment but when he is left on his own, he sometimes makes decisions that are not in his best interest.

He has a very outgoing personality which is to his advantage but he sometimes chooses to use alternative facts, instead of telling the truth. While he was in the Navy, he married a wonderful girl who taught school. I believe if he had stayed in the service, they may have stayed married. I can't be sure. When his four years was finished, he got out of the Navy and came back to Boise. He got a construction job but he was also applying for airline jobs. If he would have stayed on that course, he would have been fine but as I said before he doesn't do well when he is left to make decisions for himself. He has a tendency to look for short cuts to making "BIG MONEY."

We started hearing about burglaries in small towns around our area. Since I had a son that had stolen ID's and passports and who knows what else when he was a teenager, I began to suspect that Ron's son might be involved. I knew that Paul had sold some items to a couple of our neighbors. The police stopped by looking for him. They said there was a robbery in Weiser, Idaho a few days earlier and someone saw the two people and they suspected that our son was one of the robbers. They had convincing evidence that could link him to the robbery. We knew that he was in Seattle on a job interview with Horizon Airlines but I was scared that if it was him and he continued committing robberies someone could get seriously hurt or killed.

We couldn't live with ourselves if that happened so we told the police when Paul was scheduled to return from Seattle. He was picked up when he got off the plane and held in jail. He wasn't talking to the police. The police called us and said if he doesn't talk to them, he will go to trial and he is looking at a twenty-year sentence with no parole, if he doesn't cooperate.

Paul called us one day and I told him what the police said. I asked him if he wanted to talk to them. He said Yes. He ended up spending five years in prison and ten years on probation plus restitution to pay back. When he was released from Prison, he got a job in construction, rented an apartment and it looks like he is getting his life back together.

I am not sure if he is on top of paying his past obligations since we are still getting calls from bill collectors that are trying to get in touch with him.

He did meet a really nice woman a couple of years ago and last year they were married. I only hope that he has been honest with her about his past and if he inherits half of the characteristics from his dad, he will have a great second half of his life.

He has squandered away so much valuable time in his first fifty years. I hope and pray that he takes the talent that God has given him and he will use it benefit others.

Ron and Paul

Paul

What are the lessons I learned after 3 marriages that I wish I knew and practiced in my first marriage?

Our Life is God's gift to us and what we do with our talents God has given us is our gift to God and it will be the legacy we will leave behind. Your spouse in not your enemy

1. The couple that prays together, stays together.
2. Kiss Each Other First.
3. Comparison will kill your joy.
4. It's healthy to confess your sins to your spouse
5. It is impossible to experience marriage as God designed it without being lavish in your forgiveness of one another.
6. One of the greatest threats to a marriage is losing a teachable heart.
7. Every couple needs a mentor couple that is one lap ahead of them in the season of life
8. Never use the D-word in your marriage
9. Honor your parents (Instead of giving your parents a dust buster for Christmas, or a tie, or a pair of house slippers, give them a tribute, thanking them for what they did right.
10. Communication is a life giver of a relationship.
11. Your marriage must be built to outlast the kids.
12. As I get older, I want to laugh more with my spouse, gripe less, and be found guilty of giving her/him too much love, grace, and mercy rather than too little.
13. Become smaller, not bigger, in the lives of your adult children.
14. "I'M sorry" goes a long way to strengthen a marriage.
15. Proximity doesn't equal presence.
16. See the good.
17. Don't expect your spouse to know what is in your head or read your mind.
18. Never disrespect your spouse privately or publicly.
19. Build up your spouse.
20. LISTEN, pay attention, and not just hear.

The book Love and Respect by Emmerson Eggerichs is a must

CHAPTER 5

FAMILY LEGACY

If we know where we came from, we may better know where to go. If we know who we came from, we may better understand who we are.

What is a Family?

1. Relatives who love and care for each other deeply and put each other's needs and preference before their own.
2. A group whose love is not hindered by time, space or circumstances.

Is this the definition of your family? If not, it should be! (This is one reason there is so much dysfunction in the world. We have never learned or cared to learn how to treat each other.)

Chapter Includes:
- First Grammy experience
- Reflections of a mother
- Sibling reflection

First Grammy Experience

My son and his wife now work a lot so their four kids can be in activities which doesn't leave much time for grandma, quality parent time, and time with God.

I hope they don't have regrets later in life when Ron and I are gone and their kids are on their own and have developed their own values. Will they remember how important family and God are when they have lives of their own.

Lesson #23
Live so that when your children think of fairness, caring, & integrity, they think of you.

I remember the first time I babysat with my grandson, Sky, he was three months old. I was so excited to show him off to everyone so I put him in his car seat, buckled him in the car safety harness to leave for our adventure and started the car.

I suddenly remembered I forgot the diaper bag, jumped out of the car and ran to the house but the house key was on the car key ring so I ran back to the car. I discovered I couldn't get into the car because the car had locked when I got out.

I immediately panicked! It was 101 degrees outside but fortunately the air conditioner was on in the car. I checked to see how much gas I had. There was a half a tank. Sky was happy and laughing so he was content, at least for now. I thought about breaking the window but if I didn't do it correctly, the glass could injure my grandson and I wasn't willing to take that chance.

I ran next door to see if our neighbor had something that would work to help me get into the car. He came over with a hanger, made a loop at one end, fed it in the side of the window, managed to hook the lock and pull it up. At last the door was open and my heart could finally start beating again.

I was afraid that experience would derail my ability to be called on for future baby-sitting adventures or nominated for the "grandma of the year" award. But my son was young and took it in his stride. It didn't bother him nearly as much as it had bothered me. I am sure it aged me by at least five years.

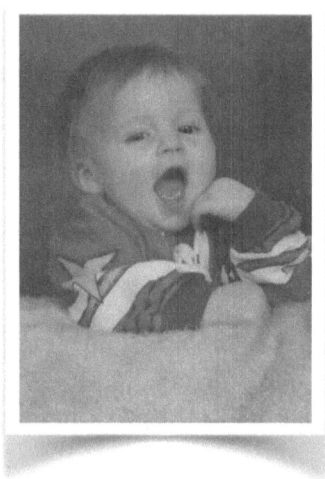

Reflection Of Motherhood

Lesson # 24
Sometimes we don't realize "When something major happens in our life it should be a wakeup call that we have been given the opportunity to "make changes in our life and the life of others in a huge way and we shouldn't throw that gift away." ...judie Dietzler

I believe the reason my son's dad picked a state so far away to take him when he kidnapped him from my home in Kansas was because he had planned to cross the border to Canada if he thought I knew where they were but the police had him put in jail before he had the chance to run.

They kept him there until we picked up Tyson and was out of the State of Minnesota headed back to Kansas.

I had to borrow the money in order to make the trip to Minnesota and once we arrived, we were told our life was in danger so we had to pick him up and drive no-stop until we were out of the state.

They talk about a Mother's Love. It is hard to explain the depth of a Mother's Love unless you have gone to the end of the earth for your child.

I have always been in the background watching over my son, even when he didn't care or didn't know it. They say my uterus almost ruptured in childbirth so I was told I should never have any more children.

I'm not sure if it was the IV I was given to induce the labor or if it was a previous surgery that caused the problem but since he was my only child I gave him all of my energy. Since he would probably be my only child, I felt I needed to be extra diligent.

It was sometimes hard to keep any eye on him because I wasn't teaching him the right way. I shouldn't have been trying to do everything myself. I should have given him to the one person that could help, God.

I stayed away from church and only prayed when I was in a jam. How pitiful is that. I prayed to God to help me get my son back or show me a sign that he wasn't supposed to be with me so I could let go and learn to live and the very next day we got a call that we could go and pick him up in Grand Portage, Minnesota.

That should be enough to get you to immediately get on your knees and from that day forward and become the best Christian you know how, but I failed miserably.

We didn't go to church when we got back from Minnesota but we did start going to church when we moved to Meridian, Idaho but we never took Tyson to Sunday School. He turned eighteen not going to church regularly, not having the opportunity to really get to know God or get saved. If he had been raised in a Christian home, he wouldn't have been roaming the streets and finding his dates on match.com. He would have instinctively known to build his friendships and dates through the church.

I've watched and worried about Tyson when he was single, working at Hewlett Packard, trying to keep his head above water financially. It was one of the most difficult times for him when he lost everything he owned in a house fire and his best friend died in the fire. He could have lost his own life that fateful night but he was working at his job instead of sleeping. Thank you, God. *(Another Miracle)*

But even today I am not sure he has stopped to think about the significance of the gift he was given and how important it is to use our gifts to benefit others. There is a fine line between helping and meddling when it comes to your adult children and it is sometimes difficult to know when one line ends and the other begins. I discovered in later years, it is a little easier to step in when they are single than when they are married without stepping on toes. I've watched and worried through his three marriages. We always want the best for our children and we hope they want the best for themselves. He would have had a much better chance if he had been raised in the church and was a Christian.

My second husband introduced Tyson to the girl that eventually became his first wife. I always felt sorry for her because she had a rough start in life and could really use someone to take her under their wing but she had a tendency to give the impression that she had all of the answers. I think she was insecure and it was a way of bluffing her way through life. But what she was lacking in self-confidence she made up for with two beautiful grandchildren that I absolutely adored. If Brandy and Tyson wanted to do anything. since they had two small kids and not a lot of money, the grandmas had the opportunity to babysit.

I bought a swing set for the kids and set it up in our backyard and I would go pick up the kids and take them to different photo studios to get their pictures taken, then we would get ice cream or French fries and come back to the house and play on the swing set. Many times, they would spend the night with me and Ron and I would take them to church the next day and then out to eat. After that we would drop them at their house.

I have so many wonderful memories of the time I spent with Tawney Star and Sky because Sky is now in the Army in Korea and Tawney Star died in the backyard swimming pool when she was four years old. Thank you, God, for allowing me those precious memories to hold onto. You knew I would need those memories because you knew what the future would hold.

Then not long after his divorce Tyson met Bunny. Her official name Bernice but everyone called her Bunny and she also had a son. They were roommates for about a year and that seemed to work out fine so they decided to make a more permanent arrangement and get married which lasted five years. My grandson had a new half-brother but he had been extremely close to his sister and he was lost after her death. Things seemed to go along fairly smoothly for a while until things got rocky with Bunny and Tyson.

He apparently thought replacing his wife was easier than fixing the relationship so he's back in divorce court and Sky has more confusion in his life. He's not doing well at home or in school. I talked to his school counselor and decided he wasn't going to make it in school if I didn't do something so I found a Psychologist and started taking him three times a week to counseling sessions and afterwards he would come to our house to eat dinner and Tyson would stop by, eat dinner and they would both go home.

Sky stayed in counseling while he was attending school at Meridian Middle school but when I met with the school guidance counselor she felt Sky would not pass if we didn't make changes so at the recommendation of his Psychologist I worked diligently to try and get an appointment with the guidance counselor at the Meridian Academy to see if we could transfer him.

They didn't have any openings for the fall term but I kept calling and begging that they sit down with us. Finally, we got an appointment with a counselor and the Psychologist, and I sat down with the Meridian Academy guidance counselor to plead our case. Sky's Mother showed up at the last minute to try and sabotage our effort but fortunately he was put on a stand-by list and right before school began for the year, we got a call that he was accepted.

If it hadn't been for my persistency in contacting the school several times a week and the help of the psychologist, I don't think Sky would have been able to get in the Meridian Academy. Meridian Middle School said they didn't think he would survive the larger school with bigger classrooms. He stayed at the Meridian Academy until graduation.

After my son and Bunny were divorced, I said "Please don't make any major life altering decisions in your first year. Give yourself a chance to heal and figure out what you want and need."

Pretty sound advice for a Mom to give. If you have any kids and you've ever given advise this will make sense. In the first year after his divorce he quit smoking (that was the good news), joined match.com, met a woman, dated her, she moved in with him, she got pregnant, he adopted her two children, they had a baby, & they bought a house. ALL IN THE FIRST YEAR. Since then they have had another baby.

Do I still worry? Every day. They both work so hard to give the kids great activities but what all kids need is quality time with their parents where they can learn great values that they can pass on to their children.

I remember one time when my son was single and didn't have kids yet I suddenly got an uneasy feeling that something was wrong. He was supposed to be with a couple of friends and hadn't shown up at the designated location so I started making calls and driving around to his usual haunts and hangouts.

No-one had seen him so I checked with hospitals and then just sat and waited. After a couple of days, he showed up and said he had just decided to go see a friend in Idaho Falls. I didn't even know he had a friend in Idaho Fall, Idaho. This was before everyone had cell phones attached to their body.

Lesson #25
"The dream of personal accomplishment is not nearly as important as God's purpose for our life."..... judie Dietzler

I have spent most of the first eighteen years of my son's life worrying about him and then before and after each relationship, with every traumatic event that I wanted to ease the pain but knew I couldn't, always hoping that he would find the peace and happiness he deserves.

Sometimes we are so busy looking for happiness that we don't realize how close it really is to us, all we need to do is stop and pay attention. The Bible says "Ask and you shall receive, Seek and you shall find." Whether you are my family or your family is in China, Russia, Washington DC or anywhere else in the world, the Bible and praying to God is the simple answer.

The dream of personal accomplishment is not nearly as important as God's purpose for our life." It took me almost seventy years & a near tragedy before I understood that Life should only be a small chapter on your way to fulfilling your true purpose. What is God's purpose for your life?

Tyson
Age 3 months

My son works way to hard!

There are advantages to being a grandma! With the first two I could drag them everywhere to have pictures taken so I have a ton of pictures.

With my next set I had to rely on my daughter in law and son to give me pictures so I don't have any except for a few snapshots. I do have one family photo that was taken a few years ago.

Do you sometimes wonder what went wrong and if you just try a little harder the relationship might survive?

I have often wondered if the courts should make it both harder to get married and harder to get divorced.

No one should be able to get married without going to marriage counseling first: It needs to include a DVD on the aftermath of divorced couples with broken homes and children that end up needing counseling in order to cope with life.

The DVD is watched in a classroom setting with a question and answer period at the end and a test. If they are going to act like kids it is time to send them back to the classroom so they can learn what it takes to have a good marriage.

Lesson # 26

The grass is not greener on the other side of the fence. It is just different......Judie Dietzler

The problems you had in this marriage will go with you because they are inside you. **For things to change, you need to change**.....Judie Dietzler

When Bunny and Tyson were married, I tried to do a lot of activities with the boys. It was important for me to stay in close contact with Sky and make sure he knew I was always there if he ever needed anything.

I stopped by to take the boys horseback riding but we ended up making it a family outing because Bunny and Tyson decided they would like to go and we had a great time.

There was a ranch where you could go no matter what your level of riding experience happened to be but I think everyone thought it would be very exciting if the person that was paying for the adventure would get the NAG, who happened to be on its last leg around the stable.

I think the nag and I happened to be the last horse and rider (you can call us that rather loosely) back into the corral. I guess I should be happy I didn't have to sleep in the wilderness that night.

I am not showing my horse because I think they hooked him back up to the buggy. I would be way to embarrassed for you to see him walking with his cane.

Our horseback riding adventure Great News! Grandma Survived!

Another great adventure was when I took my son and his son and Bunny's son to Disney land in California. My husband went along but we can usually only get my husband on the slowest of rides that a six-month-old baby might enjoy.

On the first day my son and I looked for the most exciting rides for the boys. We should have started out slower because from the second day on Nicholas (Bunny's son) and Ron (my husband) chickened out the rest of the trip and stayed at the motel swimming. What wimps.

Back to the story!

We are walking down the runway and I suddenly look up and said "Look at that, the roller coaster goes completely upside down." Everyone looked up and sure enough mickey mouse's ears were upside down. Sky immediately said "I'm not going on it."

Then it took my son and I another six hours to convince my grandson he really did want to give mickey mouse, the roller coaster a try. We even managed to get Ron and Nicholas on that one. That is probably why we couldn't budge Nicholas or Ron out of the hotel the next day.

If you look at the picture, it looks like there are only two people having fun out of the last five people in the seat.

Grandma got a workout with Sky. We would go to the Discovery Center. He was in Pals Soccer. He was my first grandchild and he had been through a lot in his young life and I wanted to make sure he had the best possible chance of success.

We also had fun on the bumper cars. We went to the Discovery Center to see their exhibits. I loved taking him places. He was fun to have around. My time with him was way to short.

Pal Soccer

DisneyLand

Bumper Cars

Discovery Center

Sibling Reflection

Between both sides of my family I have a large family but I never really got a chance to know my dad's side of the family but from the family I do know they seem to be very loving. The only family members that seemed to have a serious problem was my dad's wife and the kids that were raised by her. Since I was not around them, I have no way of understanding what their life was really like. I only know that my step-brother either shot himself or someone shot him and my dad's wife always acted like she was under the influence of either alcohol or drugs whenever I was around her.

What I do know for sure is that your environment can either BREAK YOU or MAKE YOU. The best example I know is my brother. His environment wasn't very good either. My mother kept shipping him off to a military school. Now that may have ended up good or bad. Since I've never been in a military school, I have no idea. All I know is he hated it.

But one thing that helps is if you can find a mentor which I never had until I was thirty years of age but Howard was fortunate enough to have a friend down the street and his parents became his mentors. They were very religious and Howard was religious and had a strong sense of morals, far different than our mother.

Our mother didn't practice religious beliefs but she sent all of the kids, except me, to a Christian school. I guess she was hoping that God would rub off on them and they would become upstanding citizens and religious leaders just by going to the school. Basically, she wanted the school to do the job that a parent should do, raise a bright, well educated, Christian adult that she could be proud of without her lifting a hand to help the process along.

So, Howard graduated, went on to college, got a Bachelors and Master's degree, married a wonderful woman who also has a Bachelors and several Masters degrees, had a beautiful daughter who just graduated as a Physician's Assistant and is married to a pilot. This didn't happen by accident. He worked to change his past. Our mother never lifted a finger to help anyone but herself but I believe Howard would give you the shirt off his back if he thought you needed it. I am so proud to call him my brother.

CHAPTER 6

LEGACY CAREERS

Miracle Careers

I was so fortunate to have found two wonderful careers that not only helped me change my self-esteem and life but I was able to help so many other people along the way.

My first career helped me put my past in the rear-view mirror because for the first time in my life I was surrounded by people that were positive and wanting to praise you instead of cutting through you with negative comments. For thirty years I was in a business with positive, enthusiastic, motivated, women.

My second career was a business where I had the opportunity to help many people that have emotional problems from the past that are affecting them in their present-day life. If they don't solve and heal the emotions will carry-over to their future. I helped my clients discover how to release the trauma and leave the past where it belonged, in the past.

Chapter Includes:

- **First Miracle Career.** *Mary Kay Cosmetics*
  Thanks to this career I was always home when my son got home from school and I was able to be his Cub Scout Leader and participate in all of his school functions. That would not have been possible if I had been an employee at a company.

- **Second Miracle Career** *Certified Clinical Hypnotherapist*
  My training with Mary Kay helped me understand the power of the mind and how hypnotherapy could benefit people in healing from physical and emotional trauma. It was a natural step in my evolution to healing my own body and eventually helping so many others along the way.

- *Third Miracle Business Melaleuca online wholesale Shopping*
  Toxic Free-Living: Helping individuals and families set up online shopping accounts with a USA manufacturer to purchase products at wholesale. In addition, they are able to receive discounts from over 650 additional companies through the Melaleuca Portal. What could be better than staying healthy and saving money!

The Miracle Career

A Career Built On The Principal Of The "Golden Rule" Mentors that taught me a Life-Time Of Values!

I was so fortunate to have two important business mentors at a very critical time in my life. I was asked to become a Mary Kay Consultant and it seemed like an ideal situation because I could work when my son was in school and be home with him afternoons. I had sales meeting in the evening & I asked Ila if I could bring him with me. Normally kids didn't come to sales meeting but she knew the situation so she said it would be ok. He was perfect! He sat quietly, drawing pictures on his notepad.

I advanced quickly in the ranks with the company. I became a Sales Director with Mary Kay Cosmetics in less than a year and I was newly married.

I spent a year working with Ila Burgardt, who would soon to be my National Sales Director. Ila was so good at helping me believe in my potential as a great beauty consultant. She would tell other consultants how great I was at talking to strangers and she would say "Judie is so great at talking to people, she will be happy to show you how to warm chatter recruit."

To tell you the truth, I was scared to death and I just hated talking to strangers. I was so shy, but what I hated even more was letting Ila down, so I smiled and said I would be happy to go out with them and show them how to do it. That reminds me of one of Mary Kay's sayings.

LESSON #04
"Your attitude determines your altitude. If you think you can, you can; and if you think you can't you are right."

In the end I was the winner because I became a stronger leader and working with Ila for the year before I moved to Idaho helped me believe in my abilities. I worked consistently and became a Sales Director with the company in a record eleven months, which is as fast as humanly possible. I was fortunate to train as a Sales Director with Mary Kay Ash,

In the fall my son was six years old and I decided to look for somewhere to move where I could build a strong business with my company. Over the next thirty years I didn't realize that the lessons I learned from Mary Kay would carry me though many valleys and also to the top of mountains.

I checked with my company and they said there were two states that they didn't currently have any Sales Directors, Vermont and Idaho. I chose Idaho because it was the right size, good climate and I wanted an area that would be safe for my son to grow and thrive.

Mary Kay's left hand is on my shoulder

So, we left for the adventure of a lifetime. I had lived in Kansas all of my life and now I was moving 1300 miles away to an area I had never even visited. As far as I knew it was the wilderness. My dad told me all they had were jack rabbits and sagebrush which wasn't very encouraging but we were packed and ready to go along with two of my consultants who decided to head out on this adventure with me. I was glad to have the company since my husband had gone to Idaho 3 months earlier to see if he could find work and I really didn't want to make the long trip by myself with a small child, a dog and everything we owned in a U-Haul trailer behind my car.

I was in a new location, building my Mary Kay Cosmetics business from the ground up. In my heart I knew that if I worked the business every day somehow everything would work out. I worked the business while my son was in school and if I had evening meetings, I took him with me. Even though we were miles away from my son's dad I didn't feel I could take a chance that he could get kidnapped again so I didn't leave him with a babysitter.

Over the next thirty years I didn't realize that the lessons I learned from Mary Kay would carry me though many valleys and also to the top of mountains.

Lesson #5
"Aerodynamically, the bumble bee cannot fly, but the bumble bee doesn't know it so it goes on flying anyway" Mary Kay Ash

(Since the Bumble Bee could miraculously fly because he didn't know he couldn't fly I followed the lead of the Bumble Bee along with my Idaho Team. We believed we could soar and so we did.)

Over the next five years our team achieved many great company accolades and awards. I even made it to the Idaho Statesman as the "Idaho Mary Kay Pink Lady" with a picture of me and our team Pink Cadillac. We were on a roll with our own Mary Kay training center that I shared with my three first line and five second line Directors. In addition, I had the honor of being selected to teach classes at our Annual Seminar for a number of years. (If Mary Kay said it was possible, I believed her)

Lesson #06
"Don't limit yourself. Many people limit themselves to what they think they can do. You can go as far as your mind lets you.
What you believe, remember, you can achieve". – Mary Kay Ash

Some of The Awards Our Team Won

Lesson #07
"Fear is faith that it won't work." Mary Kay Ash ***Everyone has obstacles to overcome, but those with the great faith can conquer whatever stands in the way.....*** Mary Kay Ash

I remember the first time I was asked to be a speaker at Seminar. I was thrilled but scared to death because I was basically shy. When I first joined Mary Kay the last thing I would have ever said "yes" to was talking in front of any group, and never in front of a group of several hundred. But here I was doing what I feared the most.

Lesson #08
"Courage is being Scared but saddling up anyway."

The Mary Kay years were wonderful. I developed many great friendships and I planned on retiring from my career at the ripe young age of 65 as a National Sales Director and traveling the world but sometimes the best laid plans go south.

At the height of our team greatness my personal life began to unravel. Even though my son had been kidnapped by his dad and we moved to another state I always felt he had the right to know and love both parents. I never had any anger toward his dad when he kidnapped him the first time. I realized that he had to be in a lot of pain in order to uproot himself and his girlfriend and go into hiding with our child.

Every summer I would allow our son to fly back to see his dad for a visit and he would send him back on time. When he was eleven, he got on the plane for his usual summer visit with his dad but on the day he was scheduled to return I received a call from his dad that said, "I'm not returning him."

The first thing I did was collapse on the floor in a heap of tears and sobbed for what seems like hours but then I pulled it together and went to see my attorney and explained when happened. He said since the crime didn't happen *in* the state of Idaho, we couldn't get our authorities involved but what he could do was put together paperwork for us to legally go to Missouri and kidnap my son back.

I called my brother, who lived in Kansas, and explained what happened and he immediately volunteered to drive to Missouri and kidnap him back for us, which is exactly what he did.

He went to the school my son was attending and told him he was going to take him for ice cream and then take him to his dad's. As soon as he was in the car he started driving toward Idaho. For the first couple of hundred miles he had to hold my son down to keep him from jumping out of the car but then he settled down.

A few days later they made it back to Idaho and we tried our level best to get our son back to something that seemed like a normal life.

Winning my first Mary Kay Pink Cadillac

I never asked him about his time in Missouri but I did take him to a counselor at the suggestion of the school guidance counselor. He did mention one time that his Dad was growing grass in his closet which we found out later was Marijuana.

His dad was required to appear in court and the judge told him the following, "Mr. Schmidt, I have never required this of any father in my court room before but you do not appear to be a responsible parent so I am going to impose a fine on you in order for you to have visitation rights with you son in the future." Before each and every planned visit you will deposit $3,000 into Mrs. Burns attorney's account that will be released immediately to her if your son is not returned at the agreed designated day and time."

Every year when it was time for him to visit with his dad it would once again cost me attorney fees in order to make sure I had protection in place in case my son was not returned on the scheduled time. The money wasn't nearly as important as the time spent worrying that nothing would go wrong, hoping that Dave wouldn't go off the deep end and run for it again. I didn't think I had the strength or money to chase him ONE

MORE TIME. I ended up having to sell my house, limited edition prints, plus many other items and moving from our 3000 square foot house to an 800 square foot house with one bedroom and one bath. The house was in such bad shape that there was no way I could hold sales meetings at my home which caused my business and income to suffer. Another problem that added to the financial burden was that my husband had an aversion to work. He decided since I was making money there was no need for him to work. Our next problem happened because I was making enough money that I ended up owing the IRS but didn't have cash so I had to sell artwork and jewelry I had won in order to pay the IRS bill. In addition, I had huge attorney bills to pay on a continual basis because of my ex-husband's kidnapping attempts. The problems just kept piling up.

Lesson #09
You can't stand still. You either go forward or backward. You never really fail until you stop wanting.– Mary Kay Ash

The speed of the leader is the speed of the gang. – Mary Kay Ash

(It appeared that the leader not only lost her speed, but she lost her desire.)

The next part was both good and bad when we had so many offspring Directors at one time. That is a sign that the area is growing but that was also a sign that my own unit was smaller and I would need to put things in high gear, that is a problem when you have had so many emotional hits all at one time and you're not focused on team building.

Over a period of time I was just barely keeping my head above water between worrying about my son, he was skipping classes, sneaking out of the house in the middle of the night, stealing ID cards, and trying to hang out with kids that didn't have a very good reputation. I was making payments to the IRS, trying to rebuild my Mary Kay business and team, trying to motivate my husband to get a job plus trying to sell the house to get a house with lower house payments. In the eleventh hour of nearly losing the house I managed to sell it but I had to give my real estate agent four of my limited edition prints since I didn't have the money for her commission.

We moved to a house in the east end of Boise, Idaho that was tiny and it was so filthy that the kitchen cabinet had at least three inches of dirt on the shelves where the dishes and glasses had been stored and the carpets smelled with urine from the animals using them as their litter box. I didn't think life could get any worse than this. I literally sat on the porch and cried.

What else could possibly go wrong? Ever heard "When it rains it pours"! That statement is sometimes true. We were in the house approximately two weeks when the toilet in the only bathroom broke. I couldn't afford a plumber so I called a plumbing supply store and they told me what we would need to buy and they would also instruct my husband on how to fix the toilet. I broke (no pun intended) the news to my husband that he would need to fix the toilet. He promptly told me he didn't know how to fix the toilet and my reply was, "Not yet, you don't, but soon you will."

My son was once again skipping school, hanging out with bad kids, and slipping out of the house in the middle of the night. He had a girlfriend that I didn't approve of but he kept seeing her against my wishes.

I was so worried that he would get into serious trouble so I decided to go to the police station and ask for any suggestions. They suggested that I take him to breakfast on Saturday morning and let him know that I love him but that he couldn't continue breaking our house rules. We are going to set new house rules and I am posting them on the refrigerator. As long as he lives under our roof, he needs to obey the house rules, and if he decides not to obey the rules, he needs to move out. I read them to him and gave him a copy.

I told him that if he didn't follow the house rules, I would put his things on the lawn and he couldn't stay there. He told me "I couldn't do that because he was under age."

I replied "I wouldn't want to do that but I talked to the police and they said I am your parent not your door mat and they said to let you know you have a choice, follow the rules or find another place to stay."

Then I hugged him and again reminded him that I loved him and wanted what was best for him but our house could not be a "soap opera." We went home and had a happy family existence for approximately one week before he decided that he didn't want to follow the rules. That was when I made one of the most difficult decisions of my life, to put his clothes on the front lawn and tell him he needed to find somewhere else to stay until he could decide to be part of the family and follow the rules.

When I look back, I have no idea if my son was acting out because he resented me for kidnapping him back from his marijuana smoking dad. If he wanted to live with his dad instead of me all he had to do is tell me but he never said he wanted to go live with his dad in all the years he has lived with me. It would have been painful and devastating for me but I could have lived with it if that is what it would take to make him happy. Anything would have been better than losing my career, another marriage and watching him wander aimlessly from relationship to relationship without finding his true passion in life.

My husband still wouldn't look for a job and I was still carrying the full load of the bills, the IRS, the problems with my son. I couldn't have sales meetings at my home because it wasn't in a very good neighborhood and I couldn't afford to rent a meeting room yet so it was easier to do nothing, but my team wouldn't grow if I did nothing. But that was what I decided.

Ultimately, I decided that if I was going to do everything by myself, I was literally going to do everything by myself. So, the next decision was to get a divorce. I kept all of the furniture but, of course my husband didn't have any income, so I bought him furniture for an apartment so he had a new beginning. That decision didn't motivate me to jump into my Mary Kay business either.

I should have taken Mary Kay's words below and had them tattooed on my forehead so I would remember her words morning, noon and night: (These words will carry you through the lows of life along with God.)

Lesson #10
"Don't let the negatives of life control you. Rise above them. Use them as your stepping stones to go higher than you ever dreamed possible" ......
Mary Kay Ash

I moved to another house in the same area of town that was a little nicer but still not a house that I felt comfortable holding sales meetings. My Directors tried to pull me out of my slump but I wasn't ready yet. I really appreciated their attempt at wanting me to find my way back to the dream and the team but sometimes you need to find your own way, and I had lost my motivation.

This would have been the perfect time for me to jump back in with both feet and make something happen but doubt had started creeping in because of so many back to back negatives. I didn't know how to go from where I was at that moment to regaining momentum to soar to the top.

At the time the distance seemed so over whelming and the road so very long and rocky. When I started the journey the first time, I was so much younger, with much less baggage and of course at that time I was invincible. Now I was older, supposedly wiser, less stamina, more cautious and where did all that doubt come from. Is it because I was the only fish for a long time, then the biggest fish, now there are a ton of beautiful fish in the pond called Idaho?

Miracle Careers
A New Career Is launched...not by choice, but by necessity.

Lesson #11
*If it's meant to be it's up to me....*Robert H Schuller

I didn't plan on changing careers but circumstances made the decision for me. Less than a year after I had the pain in the joints of my thumbs, I developed neurological problems so severe that I ended up resigning as a Mary Kay Cosmetics Director because I could no longer get in front of groups. Every time I had symptoms it was as if I was having a stroke.

I couldn't walk without assistance, my speech was slurred, and vision was blurred. The symptoms would last approximately two or 3 hours and then I would be fine until the next time it happened.

I went to doctors and they ran every test known to mankind and all of the tests came back normal except for the EEG. I even went to Mayo Clinic and they had me in the seizure ward, even though I told them I was not having seizures.

On the final day before I was released from the hospital, they did mention in passing that I was having "brainstem migraines" but they had no idea what was causing them or how to stop them but they did give me the name of a neurologist in Nampa, Idaho that might be able to help.

He gave me a medication for the migraines but that was only part of a solution. The next part of the solution came from me. I found that when I went to the doctor and gave him three symptoms, he gave me three prescriptions. Most of my problems were not coming from the original problem but from the side effects from all of the prescriptions.

Because of my Mary Kay sales training background for asking questions I decided to get on the computer and research. I was having so much pain and I couldn't isolate it to specific area.

How Hypnosis helped me manage my health and launch a new career:

I knew how powerful the mind was and I found a hypnosis training center in Salt Lake City, Utah. I decided to go there and train to be a hypnotherapist. At the time I wasn't thinking about careers, only about helping my own situation.

When I began my training, I was a closet smoker and for the month I was in training I smoked when we had our breaks. I was one of the class participants and the instructor helped me work through some of my past childhood traumatic issues. At the end of the month when I returned to Boise, Idaho I was still smoking. But three months later something happened.

I ran out of cigarettes and kept putting off buying more and haven't smoked again.

God created something unique when he created a human but unfortunately there isn't an instruction manual so everything that we have learned has been due to scientific evaluation or trial and error since the beginning of mankind.

The development of concepts, beliefs and practices related to hypnosis and hypnotherapy have been documented since prehistoric to modern times.

Although often viewed as one continuous history, the term hypnosis was coined in the 1880's in France, some twenty years after the death of James Braid, who had adopted the term hypnotism in 1841.

You have your conscious and sub-conscious mind. The conscious mind is the rational analytical part of your mind. (Our ability to rationalize our actions is what keeps us sane) The conscious mind is where we harbor will power.

The subconscious mind is home for the permanent memory. Every piece of data ever received through any of our 5 senses is stored in our subconscious mind for recall and review. Our permanent memory is what makes us who we truly are. We will think our next thought, act our next action and feel our next feeling based upon everything that has happened in our past.

The subconscious mind is the feeling mind. Holding in negative emotions is repression. It fills prisons, it kills and it sells a lot of medicine.

The last characteristic of the subconscious mind is that it is the protective mind. ***It will protect us from dangers, real or imagined.*** That's what phobias are all about.

My subconscious protected me in the only way it knew how to protect me at that moment when my dad died. I needed to find a way to release the emotional hurt and pain from my childhood. I felt I needed to get even because he robbed me of my childhood and the only way to do that was for me to take up his dirty, nasty habit of smoking.

It helped shorten his life, maybe it would do the same for me. After all I couldn't shout, scream or cry. He couldn't apologize. What else could I do? I didn't realize when I searched for a way to help myself, I would end up helping so many other people along the way.

Over the years I have worked with many clients that have had similar problems. They were stuck emotionally because of problems that happened in their childhood or earlier in life. *Life is a matter of perceptions. I can't change the events of their life but what I can do is help them change their perceptions of what happened.*

Sometimes they can go back to the person that they had a conflict with and they can talk and solve the situation but if the person has died, they need to discover new and different ways to have closure, and that is where I can help.

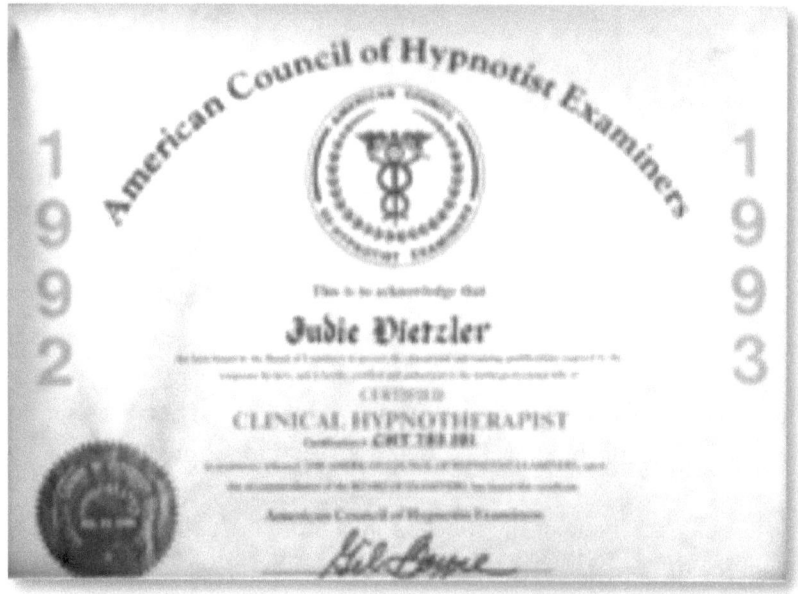

My un-expected Business……through healing

Melaleuca….The Wellness Company
In just 30 years, Melaleuca has grown from a little startup in rural Idaho to a 2 billion-dollar enterprise doing business in 19 countries around the globe. It has become one of the largest catalog and online wellness retailers in North America. And it is the largest manufacturer of consumer-packaged goods in the Northwest. Today, more than a million customers shop with Melaleuca every month.

Melaleuca's mission is to enhance the lives of those we touch by helping people reach their goals. Not just any goals, big goals. The desire to be happy. To be well in every aspect of life. That's what makes Melaleuca different. Melaleuca is The Wellness Company. By wellness, we mean complete wellness. Total wellness in four distinct but connected areas:

Your Health
It all starts with improving your health with a full line of world-class wellness products, supplements, nutrients, functional foods, and breakthrough innovations that naturally and effectively manage weight, improve nutrition, and advance health. So, you can live with vitality and purpose at every stage of life.

Your Environment
Melaleuca is on a mission to improve our environment with non-toxic, home-cleaning products that are safer for your home and allow you to live clean without the dangers of harsh, caustic chemicals. Melaleuca is a world leader in concentrated products. Products that require less water to make, less fuel to ship, and less plastic to package. They're better for the environment inside your home… and outside.

Your Finances
Melaleuca does what no other company can. Melaleuca makes it possible to improve your financial well-being, by providing a step-by-step plan

that reduces debt and increases your monthly income. Since its inception, Melaleuca has shared over $4.1 billion with families.

Your Quality of Life

In today's world one of the greatest luxuries is the ability to reclaim your time. To live life on your own terms. To pursue your passions. A Melaleuca business improves your quality of life by putting you in control of your future.

Helping People Reach Their Goals

It's a lofty ambition: helping people reach their goals. Not something an ordinary company cares all that much about. Then again, Melaleuca is anything but ordinary.

I don't sell the products. I help individuals and families that would like to buy over 400 toxic free products directly from the company at wholesale prices. In addition they are able to get additional savings at over 650 additional companies through our online Melaleuca shopping portal.

I have neurotoxicity and mold in the brain. My symptoms are so severe it is like I am having a stroke which will last approximately three or four hours and the symptoms will then slowly go away until the next time. I never know when I will have them but I have been symptom free since I removed the chemicals from my home such as cleaning products, body care, hair care, skin care and switched everything to Melaleuca.

Find out more at www.judiedietzler.com

Picture
To The Right

My Brother
And Son
At A Melaleuca
Training With
Me

The Melaleuca Store in Idaho Falls, Idaho

Picture
To the right

Melaleuca
Booth
At
A
Health
Fair

CHAPTER 7

LEGACY OF HEALING

They say that LAUGHTER and LOVE is the best medicine!

So you should begin with some reruns of "I Love Lucy" shows to get you started followed by anything else that will make you roll on the floor laughing.

Chapter Includes:

>Your Toxic Enemy...How to heal & thrive in a toxic world."
>Learning to Live "Toxic Free"
>Acupressure
>Ayurvedic Medicine
>Balneotherapy
>Biofeedback

Chiropractic
Homeopathy
Naturopathy
Reflexology
Reiki
Lifetime Vibe
The BioMat
Pets heal the heart

Learning to live Toxic-Free

I have been symptom free since 2011 but it wasn't an easy road. Every time I went to my traditional doctor and gave him/her a list of symptoms they would give me prescriptions. I would call them and say "I think the medicine is making me worse." and their comment would be "Nonsense, I'm sure you are getting better, just keep taking it."

After two or three more weeks of taking it and getting worse, crawling my way the bathroom, I stopped taking the medication and went to my computer and began researching my problem.

- I found that by removing the toxic chemicals out of my home I was able to control my symptoms which led me to write a book about Toxic Free Living.

- I began research and looking for companies in the USA that manufactured toxic free products.

- Eventually I found an online wholesale manufacturer in my home state of Idaho of toxic free products.

- I enrolled as a member and now I only use chemical and toxic free products in my home and on my body.

- I have been symptom free since 2011 which is the length of time, I have been using the toxic free products.

I say "Thank You" to God every day for my many blessings but especially the two listed below: *(Miracle)*

- He sent Mitch my way with Toxic Free Products from this wonderful Idaho Company, Melaleuca gave me my life back again.

- He gave me the wisdom to understand that by removing the toxic chemicals from my home, my life and health would improve.

- It is comforting to know that I don't need safety caps on any of the products I use.

How to heal in a toxic world

In May of 2014 I was getting ready to release my first book and I was starting a book tour throughout Idaho but sometimes plans get changed through no fault of our own.

Ron had to go into the hospital because he developed a condition called May-Thurner Syndrome which is a rare vascular condition that affects a vein in your pelvis. It occurs when a nearby artery compresses the left ilia vein.

This vein brings blood from your pelvis and legs back up to your heart. He had to have surgery to put in two stints in his groin to open the vein and restore blood flow. The doctors then put Ron on blood thinners.

So instead of doing a book tour I sat in a hospital room with Ron for the next two weeks and then took care of him once he returned home. So the book has been selling on Amazon and I am re-releasing it this year and my new publisher will start a new promotion.

Your Toxic Enemy".
How to heal and thrive in a toxic world

In this book you will learn:

- **How to recognize if your symptoms are due to toxic chemical exposure?**

- **The most common household chemicals & how to find them?**

- **How to eliminate & heal the body from toxins?**

- **How do you find the right doctor?**

I remember vividly nine years ago when my life changed because I made a decision that I felt would improve my health and life. I decided to throw out all of my cleaning products, body care, hair care, skin care, and cosmetics and "Go Green." I began reading all of the labels on my products and doing google searches.

Many of the products had known carcinogens in them and other harmful chemicals so I boxed everything up and put it by the curb for the sanitation department to take. They put a big yellow tag on it that said "hazardous waste dispose of yourself." It was to hazardous for the dump but I was using it every day in my home and on my body.

So, everything was replaced with products from an Idaho company that had toxic free products that were good for you. I don't sell the products. It is like a wholesale shopping club where you can buy products for your own personal consumption at a discount on a monthly basis. If you know someone that is in the company, they can help you get your own shopping account. To check out the shopping club go to: www.judiedietzler.com

In addition to being a member I am able to use my membership to buy products at over 650 other stores in the USA which gives me additional membership benefits. But the best part is that I stopped having the neurological symptoms three months after I started using Melaleuca's products and I am still symptom free.

The toxins are still in my body, still causing bone and joint problems. I still have the mold in my eye socket which contributes to continual problems with brain fog but I'm improving and I got my life back. I can live and go places without my husband going everywhere with me.

Whether you use this product or another product it is important to "Go Green." We Choose HEALTH. It doesn't happen by accident.

Remember Cancer is primarily caused by toxicity from lifestyle or environment. (chemical exposure)

Choose Wisely!

Lesson #27
*"The things you do for yourself are gone when you are gone, but the things you do for others remain as your legacy ...."*Kalu Kalu

Alternative Health Solutions: (No harmful side effects) Whenever possible I try to use alternative health care instead of traditional medicine. There are times when traditional medicine is necessary. If I fell and broke my arm, I would do is go to the emergency room. I also go to my primary care doctor once a year for a complete physical.

But I don't want to constantly be pumped with prescription drugs which is what I found usually happened when I went to the doctor but I found that if I went to alternative doctors, they searched for the cause of the problem instead of just working on masking the symptom with a drug. If you remove the symptom but don't solve the problem the body is so smart it will usually manifest additional symptoms in other parts of the body. I found if I didn't like the first symptom, I wasn't going to like the rest of the symptoms either. I usually improved faster if I didn't have the drugs.

Here are some wonderful alternative therapies I have used successfully that you may want to consider:

The term "alternative therapy" refers to any health treatment not standard in Western medical practice. Beyond that, complementary and alternative therapies are difficult to define, largely because the field is so diverse; it encompasses practices spanning diet and exercise changes, hypnosis, chiropractic adjustment, and poking needles into a person's skin (aka acupuncture). Technically, "alternative" treatments are used in place of conventional medicine; when used alongside standard medical practices, alternative approaches are referred to as "complementary" medicine.

More than 38% of American Adults use some form of alternative medicine.

1. Acupressure

Acupressure is similar in practice to acupuncture, only no needles are involved. Practitioners use their hands, elbows, or feet to apply pressure to specific points along the body's meridians. According to the theory behind acupressure, meridians are channels that carry life energy (qi or chi) throughout the body. The reasoning holds that illness can occur when one of these meridians is blocked or out of balance; acupressure is thought to relieve blockages so energy can flow freely again, restoring wellness. More research is needed, but pilot studies have found positive results: Acupressure might decrease nausea for chemotherapy patients and reduce anxiety in people scheduled to have surgery.

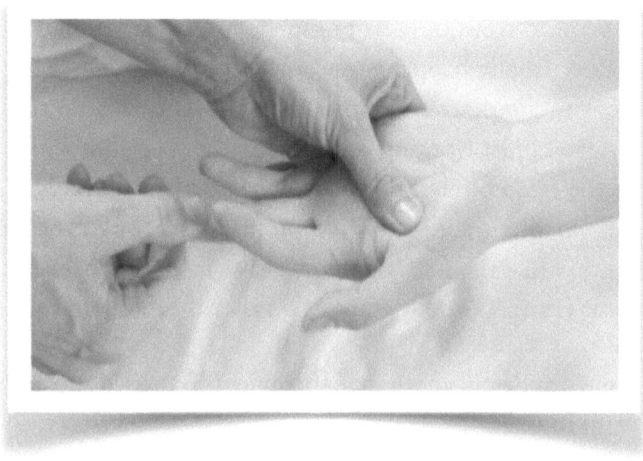

2. Ayurvedic Medicine

Also known as Ayurveda, Ayurvedic medicine originated in India and has been around for thousands of years. Practitioners use a variety of techniques, including herbs, massage, and specialized diets, with the intent of balancing the body, mind, and spirit to promote overall wellness. Studies of Ayurveda are few and far between (perhaps because the practice includes such a wide variety of treatments), so it's difficult to determine how effective it is as a treatment system (But the fact that the treatment system has persisted for so many years suggests it's got something going for it.)

3. Acupuncture

Though "acupuncture" may immediately bring needles to mind, the term actually describes an array of procedures that stimulate specific points on the body. The best-known variety consists of penetrating the skin with thin needles controlled by a practitioner or electrical stimulation, and it's currently used by millions of Americans each year. Despite its popularity, controversy over acupuncture's efficacy abounds. Some studies find it helpful for chronic pain and depression.

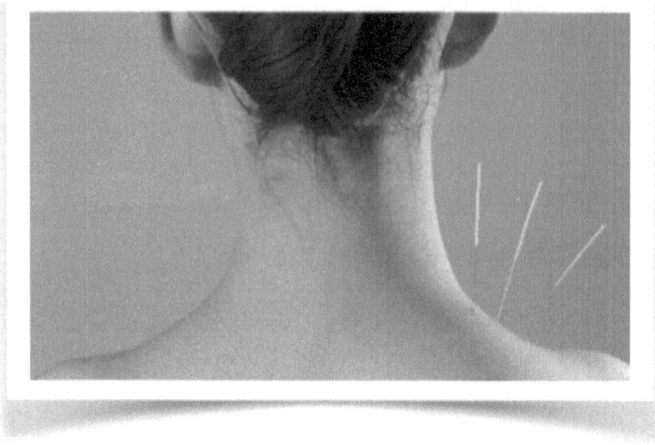

4. Aromatherapy
Aromatherapy uses essential oils (concentrated extracts from the roots, leaves, seeds, or blossoms of plants) to promote healing. The oils can be inhaled, massaged into the skin or (in rare cases) taken by mouth, and each has a specific purpose: Some are used to treat inflammation or infections; others are used to promote relaxation.

Studies suggest aromatherapy might reduce pain, depression, and anxiety, but more research is needed to fully determine its uses and benefits. I use the essential oils from Melaleuca because I know they are toxic-free.

5. Balneotherapy

Also known as hydrotherapy, balneotherapy involves the use of water for therapeutic purposes, and it dates as far back as 1700 B.C.E. It's based on the idea that water benefits the skin and might treat a range of conditions from acne to pain, swelling, and anxiety; practitioners use mud packs, douches, and wraps in attempts to reap agua's rewards.

Proponents of the therapy cite findings that water might boost people's immune systems, though research on balneotherapy's effectiveness remains inconclusive.

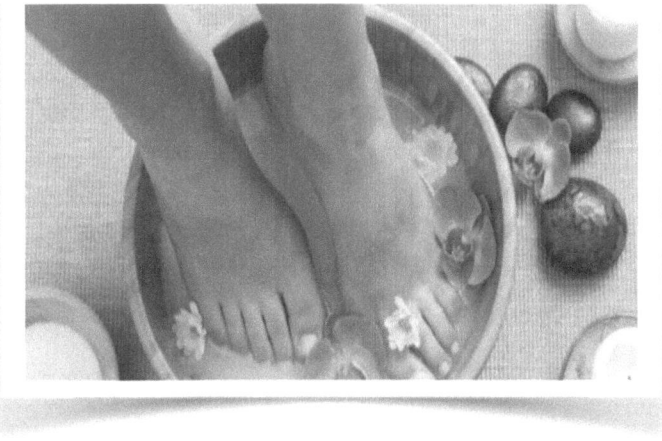

6. Biofeedback

Biofeedback techniques allow people to control bodily processes that normally happen involuntarily—such as heart rate, blood pressure, muscle tension, and skin temperature—in order to improve conditions including high blood pressure, headaches, and chronic pain. Patients work with a biofeedback therapist to learn these relaxation techniques and mental exercises. In initial sessions, electrodes are attached to the skin to measure bodily states, but eventually the techniques can be practiced without a therapist or equipment. Researchers still aren't sure how or why biofeedback works—but a lot of research suggests it does work. Relaxation seems to be a key component, as most people who benefit from the practice have conditions that are caused or exacerbated by stress.

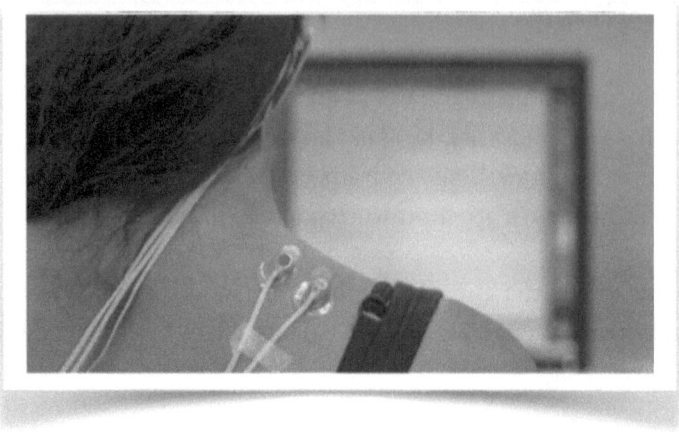

7. *Chiropractic*

Chiropractic is pretty widely accepted in the medical community, and thus qualifies more as a "complementary" medicine than an alternative one. The practice focuses on disorders of the musculoskeletal and nervous systems, including pain in the back, neck, joints, arms, legs, and head. The most common procedure performed by chiropractors is "spinal manipulation" (aka an adjustment"), which involves applying controlled force (typically the chiropractor's hands) to joints that have become "hypomobile."

The idea is that joints' movements become restricted when surrounding tissues are injured either during a single event (tweaking a muscle during a weight-lifting session) or through repetitive stress (sitting with poor posture for extended periods). Chiropractic adjustments of the affected area are intended to restore mobility and loosen the muscles, allowing the tissues to heal and the pain to resolve. Studies of chiropractic generally affirm its efficacy, with research suggesting the practice can decrease pain and improve physical functioning.

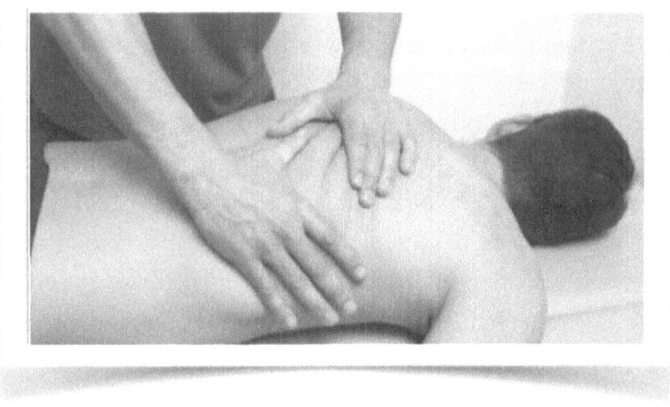

8. Homeopathy

Homeopathy functions in much the same way as a vaccine. It's based on the principle of treating "like with like," meaning a substance that causes adverse reactions when taken in large doses can be used—in small amounts—to treat those same symptoms. (This concept is sometimes used in conventional medicine, as well; for example, Ritalin is a stimulant used to treat patients with ADHD.) Homeopaths gather extensive background information on patients before prescribing a highly diluted substance, usually in liquid or tablet form, to jumpstart the body's natural systems of healing. There's some clinical evidence that homeopathy is more effective than placebos, though more research is needed to determine its efficacy.

9. Naturopathy

Naturopathic medicine is premised on the healing power of nature. Naturopathic doctors are trained in both conventional and alternative medicines, and seek to understand the cause of a condition by exploring its mental, physical, and spiritual manifestations in a given patient. Naturopathy typically involves a variety of treatment techniques including nutrition, behavioral changes, herbal medicine, homeopathy, and acupuncture. Because it involves so many different therapies, it's difficult to design studies that specifically target naturopathy's effectiveness. That said, one study that evaluated the practice for low back pain found positive results.

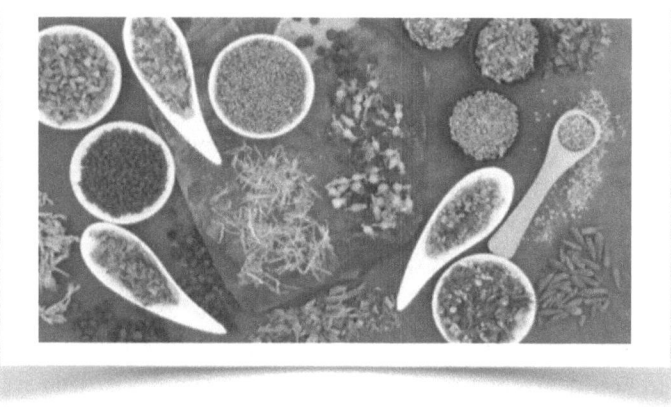

10. Reflexology

Reflexology involves applying pressure to specific areas on the feet, hands, or ears. The theory is that these points correspond to different body organs and systems; pressing them is believed to positively affect these organs and a person's overall health. (For example, applying pressure to a spot on the arch of the foot is believed to benefit bladder function.) A person can either use reflexology on her or his self, or enlist the help of a reflexologist. Millions of people around the world use the therapy to complement conventional treatments for conditions including anxiety, cancer, diabetes, kidney function, and asthma. Some studies have found that reflexology can improve respiratory function in breast cancer patients, reduce fatigue, and improve sleep—but other studies have reached less definitive conclusions.

11. Reiki

Reiki is a form of energy healing based on the idea that a "life force energy" flows through everyone's body. According to this philosophy, sickness and stress are indications that life force energy is low, while energy, health, and happiness signify a strong life force. In a Reiki session, a practitioner seeks to transfer life energy to the client by placing their hands lightly on the client's body or a slight distance away from the body (Reiki can also be performed long-distance). The purpose is to promote relaxation, speed healing, reduce pain, and generally improve the client's wellbeing. For the most part, there's no regulation for Reiki practitioners. Studies of the practice's efficacy are varied: Some find therapeutic touch to be an effective form of treatment; some don't.

Disclaimer: The information above is only preliminary. It's always advisable to contact a medical professional before undergoing any form of conventional or alternative medical treatment. This information was part of an article that was read and approved by Greatest Experts Dr. Mike Reinold and Dr. Phil Page.

The following are alternative modalities that I use daily and wouldn't be without for continued health benefits.

The Lifetime Vibe:

Whole Body Vibration is an innovative, safe, and effective exercise option. It is the use of a moving platform at specific frequencies and amplitudes to superimpose vibration on normal functional strengthening exercises. Like no other exercise, whole body vibration works directly through the nervous system creating a significant increase in the normal physiological responses of the body to exercise. Here are a just few of the challenges that the Lifetime Vibe benefits:

Osteoporosis	Stress	Dizziness
Balance	Incontinence	Hip Pain
Lower Back Pain	Muscle Strength	Cellulite.
Parkinson's Disease	TMJ	Neck Pain
Planter Fasciitis	Varicose Veins	
Lymphatic System	much more.....	

To find out more about Lifetime you can go to www.lifetimevibe.com and enter the code: Judie

How does whole body vibration work?

The vibration platform produces vertical vibrations from a side-alternating rocking movement which simulate walking. Our body reacts to this natural stimulus with an involuntary "stretch reflex" body reaction. This is the that occurs when the doctor hits your knee or elbow with a reflex hammer. As a result of the rapid stretch to the muscle tendon caused by the tap of the hammer (the oscillating platform), the muscle contracts to oppose the stretch.

The vibration, frequency, amplitude, and resulting acceleration create thousands of these muscle contractions in a matter of just minutes. Without being aware of it, when we are in motion our muscles are always able to keep us upright and balanced. This natural reaction is what's being employed with whole body vibration.

Every time the plate moves, your body has no choice but to respond; rebalancing you by engaging and disengaging your muscles numerous times per second. The best part is, because the reactions are so quick and involuntary, it actually feels good! The sensation is more like a massage or gentle stretching- nothing like pounding through several sets at a gym. Depending on the speed, your muscles will contract up to 30 or more times per second. Energy is safely and effectively transferred to your body, stimulating every cell, your muscles, your bones and your soft tissue. Contractions occur in nearly 100% of the muscles, in comparison to 40-50 % involvement in traditional exercise. As a result of this exceptional high number of contractions a wide array of benefits is experienced. **Can you exercise all of your muscle groups?** Yes, the vibration does not discriminate between different muscle groups, for example, quadriceps and hamstrings. The muscles work together as you exercise. The vibration is highest in the body parts that are closest to the platform. The vibration dampens as it travels up the body. This leads to the ability of the body to carry off waste products much faster, leading to increased peripheral circulation.

The claims of benefits achieved from vibration have been extensive. Can it really be true that you can achieve such wide & varied benefits?

Yes, the claims are made as a result of research from over 40 universities worldwide. More the 978 articles on whole body vibration are listed in the US National Library of Medicine. The numbers change weekly as this technology becomes more and more accepted and more research is concluded by universities, chiropractic, physical therapy, and sports enthusiasts. The medical community is now beginning to embrace whole body vibration.

BioMat

Another successful and phenomenal Alternative Health Product that I use daily with both myself and with clients is the BioMat

How does the BioMat deliver far infrared rays and negative ions to the human body?
The BioMat stimulates ion channels by producing negative ions that deliver energy to the cells of the body. The top most layer of the BioMat is constructed of super conducting channels of pure amethyst, which allow the far infrared rays and negative ions to penetrate the body as far as seven inches.

How does amethyst quartz enhance ionic and far infrared ray therapy?
Amethyst's healing properties have been acknowledged and celebrated for centuries by ancient scientists, healers and others. Now, modern science has confirmed the highly conductive properties of this remarkable mineral. Amethyst crystals offer the most consistent and powerful delivery of far infrared light waves, and ionic effects to the human body.

Can the BioMat be used during yoga and meditation?
Yes, the BioMat is a perfect addition to yoga practice and meditation, because it supports deep, muscle relaxation, increases blood flow for

improved local circulation where applied, and provides a warm, soothing environment to facilitate improved mental peace and serenity.

Is the BioMat easy to use?
Yes, even though the BioMat is a certified medical device, it is very easy to self-administer calibrated treatment. The computerized control panel is intuitive to use, and comes with a simple set of instructions.

When will I start to see results from my BioMat?
Every person's experience with the BioMat is different. Many people achieve immediate relief from certain pain and discomfort, right away. For others, it will take a few weeks before the deep-penetrating treatment begins to bring relief. Because the BioMat's far infrared rays penetrate deeply into the body and promotes our natural state of health and balance, it can be used to treat a wide range of health issues. Release stress by relaxing your muscles and enjoying soothing Far Infrared ray heat, simply lying on the BioMat promotes a feeling of well-being for a healthier mind and body.

The US FDA's Medical Device 510K indications for use are as follows:

What specific conditions and symptoms can the BioMat treat?

- Relaxation of muscles
- Increase of local circulation where applied

Temporary relief of:

    Minor joint pain and stiffness
    Joint pain associated with arthritis
    Soothes and relaxes
    Supports the immune system
    Improves sleep (if associated with pain relief)
    Reduced inflammation (where applied)
    Minor muscle pain
    Increased tissue oxygen (due to increased circulation where applied)
    Muscle Spasms

Minor Sprains
Minor Strains
Minor Muscular Back Pain
Reduces Stress and Fatigue

The BioMat was used in a Japanese clinic for the comfort of terminally ill cancer patients that were sent there to a hospice retreat for their final days.

The BioMat was used as one of the comfort tools. They not only were comfortable, after continued use of the BioMat the doctors could not find any signs of the cancer so the patients were released to go home and enjoyed the rest of their healthy days with their families.

I use the BioMat with clients that have cancer also, except for brain cancer.

There are two things that cancer hates:
1. Alkalinity
2. Heat.

Cancer loves the following:
1. Sugar

If you want to eliminate Cancer give it what it hates and eliminate what it loves!

Pets heal the heart

Baby (White with a little black on her ears) only barked twice in twenty years when I was too slow giving her a treat. 6 pounds and adorable.

Teddy Bear on the left was a great little guy who loved french fries. My husband said he was the smartest dog her had.

PePeLePew gets so excited when we come home that he yodels. When we first received him as a gift from my son and daughter-in law I thought he would make a great therapy dog but now I think he might just need a lot of therapy. But we adore him

PooBear is a cute little white Maltese. His owners died and he needed a home so we kept him until we could find someone to love him.

I gave him to a client on disability that had lost her dog. He was a real lap dog.

CHAPTER 8

LEGACY OF FRIENDSHIP

What is Friendship? It isn't about who you've know the longest. It's about who walked into your life and said I'm here for you, and proved it!

I didn't have the opportunity to have close friends until I joined a sorority after I married my first husband because I was so busy working. You can contact the Chamber of Commerce in your area or do a google search for business women's sororities.

If you want to combine the fun of a friendship organization with community service there are many service organizations that you can join that would love to have both your expertise and energy.

Here are some of the social organizations that I have had some crazy and wacky fun with over the years & they have also participated in community service but their primary objective is to **HAVE FUN.**

Fight for you
Respect you
Include you
Encourage you
Need you
Deserve you
Stand by you

Where it all started.......

In 1931, during the Great Depression, there was a need for an organization that could bring women together and expose them to a social, cultural and educational climate that was not available in those difficult times.

Beta Sigma Phi was created out of this need. It did not take long before Beta Sigma Phis were helping others.

- Members worked together to raise $22 million in war bonds during World War II.

- Membership in our organization provides opportunities to contribute to our community, develop lifelong friendships, and polish leadership skills.

- Our members raise more than $3 million for our local charities and donate over 200,0000 volunteer hours in an average year.

- Beta Sigma Phi is dedicated to helping women fulfill their lives. Whether our fulfillment lies in making new friends, helping our local community, or just finding time for us-the choice is ours. I joined Beta Sigma Phi in 1968 when I was first married and it was a new & different experience. My brother & sisters were small when I left home so I didn't have a sibling relationship.

I had two girlfriends growing up but one died before I got married & the other moved out of state. I was so quiet & shy that I had never developed friendships with women so this was a new & different experience. They had cultural events, social functions, valentine balls, teas, picnics. It was a way to maintain a business life if you worked outside the home, raise a family but have a night out a couple of times a month with the girls & have fun.

In addition, we also did Service projects in the community that helped women, children & the elderly. Beta Sigma Phi is a wonderful experience for a woman, at any age. As I have traveled around the country without a doubt you never walk alone. You always find a Beta Sigma Phi friendly face to walk beside you.

I began my membership as a member of Beta Sigma Phi in Wichita, Kansas & absolutely loved it. I had never had girlfriends except in school until I joined sorority.

My husband was a computer expert for IBM and his best friend's wife was in a chapter and invited me to join. As you can see, we had a lot of fun.

We had a Luau and my husband was one of the hula dancers.

I also joined the "Swinging Phi's" and we sang at many functions across the city.

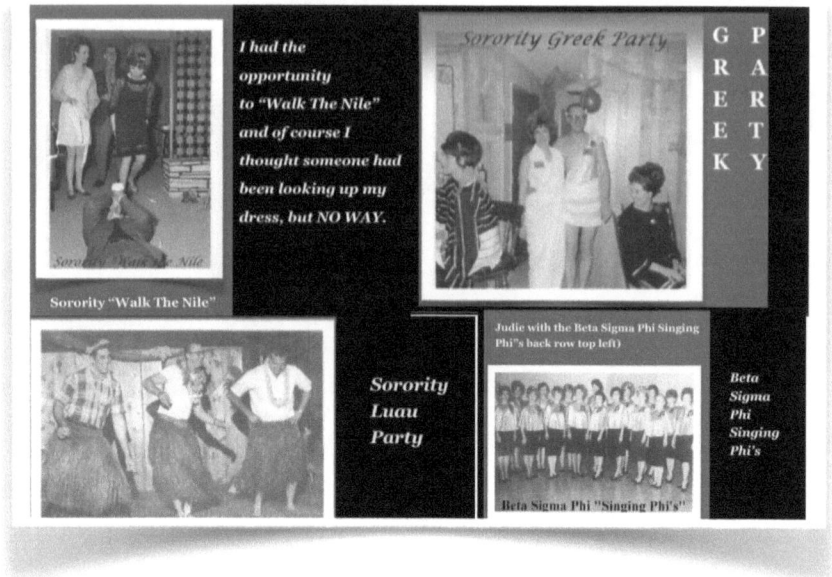

Then I moved from Kansas to Idaho and there was a long period of time that I wasn't part of sorority because I was so busy as a Sales Director building a Cosmetics business in Idaho and bringing in the only income in our family. But after I married Ron, for the first time in over forty years I had real stability in my life. I could travel and take continuing education classes with wonderful people like Deepak Chopra, and Dr. Andrew Weil, Oprah and many more. I was also able to find Beta Sigma Phi in my community and once again joined a chapter and met some wonderful new friends.

Lesson #28
"Walking with a friend in the dark is better than walking alone in the light."

I think this portrays wonderfully what Beta sigma Phi means to its members. In my association with Beta Sigma Phi I have seen Friends who have unselfishly supported, encouraged, loved and cherished each other through both happy times and times of sadness and loss.

To me this proves that to be a success in a profession is admirable, but *to be a success in friendship is a treasure.* I think that's first and foremost what Beta Sigma Phi represents, women lifting up other women in friendship, encouraging them to give the world and each other their very best. I'm proud and delighted to be an International Honorary Member of Beta Sigma Phi.

Long live the Sisters of Beta Sigma Phi!

My best,
Earlene (a testimonial from one of our long time BSP members)

Beta Sigma Phi Convention

Examples of fun and friendships: Sometimes you just need to be a little crazy!

Members Promoting Founders dressed as penguins

Legacy of Friendships-*part 2*
Build a Legacy Through the Strength of Friendships

Red Hat Society was created to connect like-minded women, make new friends & enrich life through the power of fun & friendship. We reshape the way women are viewed in today's culture by promoting freedom from stereotypes & a positive Hattitude.

We are very lucky to have such a wonderful friend as Queen Kate as our head fun loving "Queen" of Red Hatter.

Lesson #29
A friend is a cheerleader when you win, a counselor when you lose, a confidante when you need to share, and a clown when you're feeling blue.

Red Hat Society members gather locally in groups, known as chapters, simply for fun. We support one another in every life stage from all corners of the globe:

We are reshaping the way women are viewed in today's culture by promoting, not only fun and friendship, but freedom from stereotypes and fulfillment of goals and dreams.

Fitness is the foundation on which we base healthy, rewarding lives. Red Hat Society naturally promotes positive Hattitudes.

What is a FRIEND?

- *A friend is someone who you think your life would be different if they didn't exist.*

- *A friend is someone who NEVER leaves you out, you are ALWAYS included when you are with them.*

- *A friend is there for you, no matter what.* Does this describe your friend? *If* not, maybe they are not a real friend and you need to reevaluate the friendship.

- *Are you the topic of their gossip?* Maybe you should re-evaluate the friendship.

- *A true friend never gossips at your expense and they will defend you to the end.*

Legacy Of Friendships-*part 3*

My friendship with the "Red Hat" Members grew into another wonderful group of friends. We called ourselves the *"Divas"*

There were ten of us and we started out as a group that met once a month to discuss things that were happening in the world and answered questions for a think tank and sent them back to a government group.

After a few years we decided that our answers weren't making a difference in changing the world so we decided to go a different direction. It was time to kick up our heels and have fun and additional girlfriend bonding time. We took turns picking different area events and projects that we could grow and gain new experiences. Along the way the friendships also strengthened as well.

Lesson #30
Friends walk in when everyone else walks out.

We started with ten crazy Diva's; our original friendship began in our Red Hat Ravishing Ruby Group. I never had friends with women for the first half of my life. It has never been easy for me to just hang out. I've always been so goal oriented that I felt every get together had to have a beginning. Middle, and end. I felt that life was too short not to have an end game and a plan of action.

I felt God gave us only so many hours here on earth and we needed to make it count. That is why I have always admired Oprah because she has the same twenty-four hours that the rest of us have but she is making an impact in the lives of so many people. She has Integrity and honesty and she is a woman with compassion and has a mission. She probably knows how to have fun but not when she is laser focused on her mission of making a difference in the world.

I've always looked at hanging out as something you do when you are too old to make a difference in the world.

Lesson # 31
Look for friends that bring out the best in you.

But I have learned to let my hair down a little or take it off in some cases when I decided to wear my Christmas tree instead of put it up in my house like the picture shows.

Lesson #32
A true friend loves you even when it seems like you've gone off the deep end!

Judie & Ron at Halloween Party

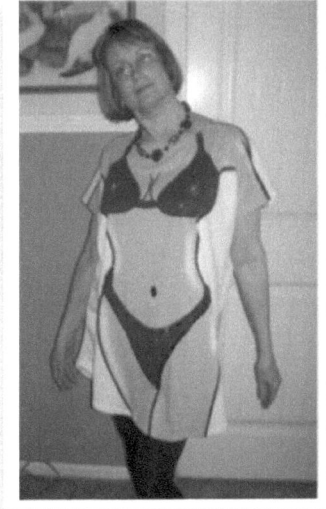
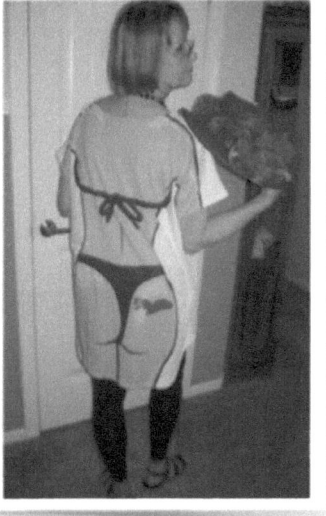

Diva

Looking back, I sometimes miss those wonderful Mary Kay days but I believe that God knew best because he sent me in a new direction and his plan must be much bigger. The road has been rocky and there have been many new lessons along the way.

But now I have a husband that promised to love and take care of me forever and he has been doing that for the past thirty years. I haven't had to worry about a roof over my head or basic necessities so I have been able to pursue many dreams and adventures throughout the years.

Since I don't have the heavy responsibilities, I was able to let my hair down and occasionally take it off.

Lesson # 33
"Age Is Insignificant; How you Live is Not".....

I would like to share something about friendship that I have learned over the years. *If you have friends that you value and are important to you treasure them and don't take them for granted. Don't use them or abuse them and above all don't gossip and talk about them to other friends under any circumstances. Keep your mouth shut and honor the relationship.*

If you start sharing little bits of information, no matter how *unimportant you think it maybe you are not honoring your relationship and little by little your friendship will die.*

I have been a Sales Trainer of women for over thirty years and in that time, I have seen how easy it has been for so many people to engage their mouth before they engage their brain and somehow they don't think about the trail of destruction they have the potential to leave behind when they speak without thinking.

I'll share some examples:

In approximately 2009 after having been on the City Council of for Beta Sigma Phi I was asked to be on board to help with the citywide convention for the next year. It wasn't something I was particularly excited about because I was already on the board of two non-profit organizations but two of the ladies were close friends so I said I would do it, which I eventually regretted.

I enjoyed myself most of the time but two or three of the ladies had the tendency to gossip and give their opinion about the people that were not present and people in other chapters plus share the latest news about everyone.

I would have much preferred not knowing the information because I always felt if they were eager to talk about what was going on in everyone else's life they wouldn't hesitate to share what was happening in my life and if there wasn't anything happening, they might help develop some juicy news.

So, I was thrilled when we were finished with the convention. I didn't realize that I was violently ill during the convention and as soon as it was completed, I rushed to the doctor and he put me in the hospital for kidney surgery.

I did go to Mexico with the convention board members but I was so unhappy for most of the trip it was all I could do to count the hours until we got back home because most of the board members did everything to make me feel unwelcome.

I would have never gone on the cruise but I didn't know how to back out gracefully. The Beta Sigma Phi motto wasn't working on the Mexico trip but I have traveled across the nation and have some wonderful Beta Sigma Phi sisters.

What is so sad is that both of my friends that were the reason I said yes to going on the cruise in the first place are no longer with us. They both died of cancer in the past few years, one in her eighties and the other in her fifties. The convention was in 2009 and this is 2019. We never know how long we have with our friends or how long we have to make things right with the world.

EVERYDAY MIRACLES

Diva

Another Diva trip: Somewhere in the beginning of our getting to know you friendship Diva trips we had a couple of interesting encounters.

Margaritaville might have been our first trip together to McCall, Idaho. We decided it would be wonderful and refreshing if we put together a big pitcher of margaritas. As we were getting the ingredients together Norva piped up and announced that she was an expert at making margaritas and she would be happy to take over the project so we stepped aside and she started tossing the ingredients into the blender like a pro.

Immediately upon finishing with the last of the items she hit the blender button like the expert she claimed to be and sure enough all of the contents of the giant blender sailed through the air onto the cabinets, walls, counter, floor and nearby participating surprised ladies. Three of us sailed across the kitchen, one grabbing the blender lid and two grabbing glasses hoping for extra beverage.

Off went the blender, salvaging the remainder of the margaritas and over the next hour we scrubbed and cleaned every nook and cranny of the kitchen, then finally settling down to enjoy our tasty, refreshing margarita.

Diva adventure remembered.............

Another time we were headed to McCall, Idaho to the cabin.

Can you tell we really like the cabin and McCall? This time Linda couldn't go. I had a friend that had this life-sized blow-up rubber doll. We had taken her to a sorority convention a couple of years earlier so I asked if I could borrow her. We took the clothes Linda had planned to wear on the trip and every time we went to bed or out anywhere, we changed her clothes and took her with us. On one such adventure we went to a street fair and a couple of guys fell in love with her so we kept passing her back and forth across a fence so they could kiss her.

One day we went huckleberry picking and Linda also picked a bucket of huckleberry's so she was very useful but she didn't pay her fair share of the gas or food so she may have been a little bit of a tight wad. But she was a lot of fun. We took a vote and decided that we would be happy to take her any time she wanted to go along for the ride.

CHAPTER 9

LEGACY OF SERVICE

The discussion of leaving a legacy is something I have thought about over the last few years after losing several close friends.

The idea of leaving a legacy is the need or the desire to be remembered for what you have contributed to the world.

In some cases, that contribution can be so special that the universe is unalterably changed. Most of us will leave a more modest legacy that doesn't necessarily change the world but does leave a lasting footprint that will be remembered by those whose lives you touched.

You hope your life matters in some way. I know I do.

Here are 5 ways to Leave a great Legacy:
1. *Support the people & causes that are important to you.*
2. *Be Inspirational & Influential in touching the lives of others.*
3. *Share your blessings with others.*
4. *Be a Mentor*
5. *Pursue Your Passions & share with others/they are part of your legacy*

This chapter includes the following service:

- *Soroptimist International*
- *Project Kids*

Soroptimist International of Boise

Lesson #34
Kind works costs little but accomplishes much

Spirit of service
What did I learn from Soroptimist?

I learned the value of commitment and service to a worthwhile goal. When you are involved in helping other people and putting their needs and interest as your number one goal there is no room for selfishness and being self-centered. People that are "Me Centered" don't last long in the world of Community Service.

I found there are so many needs in the world and not enough community minded people to help. I discovered that when you have like-minded women with a common goal you can move mountains. I was fortunate to be part of such a great group of movers and shakers that outwardly appear to be ordinary but all have extraordinary abilities and talent. You seldom hear their name but they are quietly changing our community & the world.

EVERYDAY MIRACLES

Rake Up Boise

Jailbird for Charity

March Of Dimes

A legacy of giving back to seniors and foster children

The principal goal of the project is to help the indigent elderly who reside in local care centers meet their clothing and personal care needs. Many individuals helped by this program either have no close relatives or have outlived the rest of their family.

This project helps build relationships. Care centers are canvassed for information on residents' needs and wishes. The lists are published in the local newspaper and during the week following publication, telephones are staffed by Soroptimists to take calls from the public, each adopting an oldster from the list.

Packages are brought to a collection point. They are labeled, sorted, and bagged according to care center. In prior Christmas seasons we delivered 175-200 large bags of gifts; each facility is visited at least three times per week during December.

Now the donations have increased to such quantities that we are not able to do the deliveries and the nursing homes come by several times to pick up the bags of gifts.

The oldsters Christmas gift project has been a cornerstone of Soroptimist/Boise service for over 59 years, and is our "signature" event in the community.

Soroptimist on Channel 7 Promoting the senior Cctizen (oldster) and Foster children Christmas gift giving program. My husband (Ron) and I are Mr. and Mrs. Santa.

Marian Warren and I were in the Idaho Statesman promoting the Christmas gift giving program.

EVERYDAY MIRACLES

JUDIE DIETZLER

Soroptimist March of Dimes Participation

I was asked to participate in the March of Dimes "Bail me out of jail" for the March of Dimes babies.

One of my Soroptimist friends, Sharon, was my Sheriff who handcuffed and arrested me. The squad car picked us up and off to jail we went. However, our jail was a soft padded booth at the Outback restaurant complete with a gourmet lunch. Once we were finished eating and we had raised money from friends to spring us out of the slammer there was a chance we would be released. However, there were a few that wanted to double the amount of money raised if the outback and March of dimes would keep us in lock-up for the week-end.

Fortunately, our die-hard friends (maybe 2) and our husbands came through with the needed funds and we were released.

March of Dimes leads the fight for the health of all moms and babies. We believe that every baby deserves the best possible start. Unfortunately, not all babies get one. They are changing that.

For 80 years, March of Dimes has helped millions of babies survive and thrive. They are building on that legacy to level the playing field for all moms and babies, no matter their age, socio-economic background or demographics.

They support moms throughout their pregnancy, even when everything doesn't go according to plan. They advocate for policies that prioritize their health.

They support radical improvements to the care they receive. And they pioneer research to find solutions to the biggest health threats to moms and babies.

What began with President Franklin D. Roosevelt's personal struggle with polio led to the creation of the National Foundation for Infantile Paralysis, better known as March of Dimes, and ultimately a cure for the disease.

With that success behind them, they began to focus on fighting birth defects, premature birth and infant death with innovations like newborn screenings & surfactant therapy; education for medical professionals & the public about best practices; and lifesaving research.

They provided comfort and support to families in NICUs & advocated for those who needed them most, moms and babies. Soroptimist, including Sharon and I were happy to be part of the March of Dimes fundraiser to help in the many areas that March of Dimes is helping mothers, babies, and families.

Project Kids

Another project that is near and dear to my heart is "Project Kids". Project Kids began in the year 2000 by the Women's Ministries at Valley Shepherd Church with a desire to help the children who had specific needs at the Meridian Elementary School. They wanted to make a difference in their lives. They contacted the school counselor who with the help of the school teachers identified the children in need. They served a chili luncheon to the business community and raised close to $1000. The teachers that year requested new socks, underwear and laundry detergent for their students. This chili luncheon developed into an annual dinner and auction held at Valley Shepherd Nazarene church every fall.

In January 2014 Project Kids joined the Meridian Food Bank with the goal of reaching more businesses and community members to raise funds for our children. Their mission was to work in coordination with the Meridian Food Bank and help provide basic needs for area low income families.

In 2015 Project Kids became their own 501 c 3, organization, appointed an executive board and held the dinner and auction at the West Ada School District building in Meridian, ID. By becoming a stand-alone charity, Project Kids hopes to attract new sources of income, promote the organization to new audiences, and make an even greater financial impact working with West Ada school district low income families.

Heritage Grove Community purchased two tables and won some wonderful auction items at the event.

My Red hat group also had a table and won great items. We had a lot of fun and it made me really appreciate my friends.

All you give into the lives of others comes back into your own 100-fold!

CHAPTER 10

LEGACY LIFE LESSONS

Life Lessons

This chapter is some of the lessons I have learned over the years I've learned through the road of "Hard Knocks"

- I've learned that it takes years to build up trust, and only seconds to destroy it.

- I've learned that it's not what you have in your life but who you have in your life that counts.

- I've learned-that you can do something in an instant that will give you heartache for life.

- I've learned that either you control your attitude or it controls you.

- I've learned-that sometimes when I'm angry I have the right to be angry, but that doesn't give me the right to be cruel.

- I've learned-that we don't have to change friends if we understand that friends change.

- I've learned-that two people can look at the exact same thing and see something totally different.

- We are always free to make choices, but we are not free from the consequences of those choices.

Chapter Includes:

- Our Actions Speak Louder Than Words.
- Teaching by example
- A lesson on anger

Your past does not determine your future. You alone determine your destiny with the help of God. You have the ability to leave behind a worthwhile legacy. **What do you choose?**

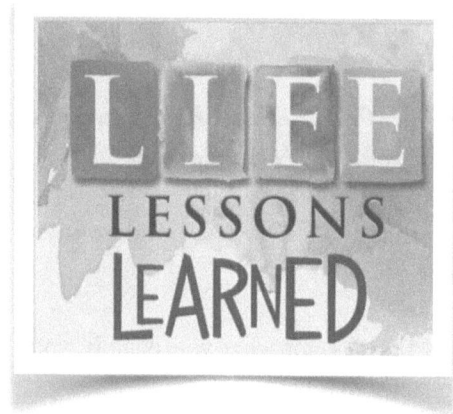

Our Actions Speak Loud

Lesson #12
Actions Speak Louder Than Words ..... Abraham Lincoln

Writing on the pages of this book has given me time to think about the past including conversations with neighbors. We always want the best for our children and I am no different. It would have been my desire for my son not to follow in my footsteps but to do it the right way. You don't just turn to God when you are desperate & ask for help.

You consult with him daily so you will make the right decisions & I can't think of a more important decision than the person you want to spend the rest of your life with. Ask God for his advice.

I look back on my two previous daughter-in-law's & would I have selected them for my son? No!

Neither one attended church nor were Christians but both had good qualities.

Brandy gave me two beautiful grandkids & with both Brandy & Bunny I had plenty of time to spend with the kids to bond & influence them while they were young. We were able to go places and have fun together. I will always remember all the fun we had.

I also remember my Mother-In-Law & Ron's cousin. Both lived in Chicago, Illinois. Betty was a ninety-two-year-old spit-fire and I enjoyed her. Both Betty & Ron's cousin Sue would call & say:

"Hi Ron, how are you," After a minute of small talk they would say "Is Judie there?"

Finally, after a few years of this Ron said to me "I wonder if they know I'm in the family." I told him that I am sure they know he's in the family but the problem is he doesn't have a conversation with them.

He only gives one-word answers and it is hard to talk to someone that doesn't talk back. That seemed to satisfy him.

I always made sure we stayed in touch with Ron's mother & went to see her often. I felt it was my place to make sure she was ok. We called. If she needed something either Ron's cousin took care of it or I would make sure it was taken care of for her.

When she passed away, we gave her the memorial service that she had requested at the church she had attended for years. She had been a resident of her retirement community for approximately seven years so she was no longer in contact with her friends from Wheaton, Ill.

The church where we had Betty's service was on a hill & there were approximately fifty steep steps from the driveway to the front entrance doors of the church.

Since Betty was ninety -two you won't be surprised to find out that her pall bears were anywhere from seventy to eighty years of age. Another fact about them was that they all had knee or hip replacements. As they are about to carry Betty down the long flight of stairs the two lead pall bears started to lose their balance due to weak knees and Betty is on the verge of sailing down Michigan Avenue airborne without the assistance of the Hurst. Fortunately, a couple of young men standing close by jumped into action and saved Betty from a fate worse than death, being crushed by a semi.

In Chicago they always have food following weddings and funerals. They must love to eat. They had a nice luncheon and we shared Betty's tribute video. What is so sad is that a few years ago Betty's daughter went to a Psychologist and he supposedly told her she should divorce her Mother so that is literally what she did. All of her life her Mother spoiled her rotten, sent her to a private school, did everything for her, and they were very close. But at some point, she started to see a Psychologist, decided her dad was an alcoholic and that her family was dysfunctional and no longer wanted to have any contact with her mother or her brother. (most families do have some level of dysfunction but you don't usually cut them out of your life because of it. You just shake your head and give them a hug, but not Ron's sister.) So she wouldn't even show up at her mother's bedside when she was dying. How do you treat someone so badly? I don't do that to my mother and she watched me as I was being sexually abused for years. Her Mother was one of the nicest people I met. I loved going to Chicago and spending time with her. They say you reap what you sow.

Lesson #13
How You Treat Your Parents Is How Your Children Will Treat You.....
quote by Judie Dietzler

Many of my neighbors are single or widows and they say that their sons are not always on top of things but their daughter-in-law is wonderful. They have said that their sons don't always pay close attention but his wife is always calling and stopping by to check to see if they need anything. They have been instructed to stay off ladders and let the family help if they need to reach anything that is on a top shelf or in a closet. It is better to be safe than sorry. If you fall when you are in your twenties you bounce back with ease but if you are in your seventies it takes a lot longer and sometimes it can be fatal.

It is so important to have a strong support system around you. If you don't have a supportive family then it is time to find another support system. I have some wonderful friends in my community and my church plus a dear friend that lives across the field from me. I discovered that I wouldn't be able to count on family when my husband was in a near fatal car accident and I had two falls that caused a traumatic brain injury. But we do have wonderful friends that are supportive.

In many towns there are non-profit groups that also help if you need help getting to doctors or errands, etc. Many church groups also are able to help. You can look for help by doing google searches in your area for Nazarene Churches and Jesus Christ of Latter-Day Saints. I am sure there are other churches that have groups that help. I am familiar with both of these churches because they helped when my granddaughter died.

I was talking to my son one day and I asked why it is that he is the only one that answers the phone when I call. His response was: When his wife's mom or dad calls, he doesn't answer the phone because they only want to talk to his wife anyway & when I call, I only want to talk to Tyson so no one else answers the phone. I could hardly believe my ears. He is part of their family & Chris is part of my family. How do you participate as part of a family if you don't communicante?

They need to understand that once you say "I do" you are saying "I do" to an entire family & it is your responsibility to be part of the entire family, not just put a little cocoon around your individual household & ignore the rest of the family. That's not how family works. When my husband was in critical condition, I didn't call them because they have never helped with anything else I have asked for so I did not plan on asking them to help with something so important.

If they really wanted to help, they would have showed up & said" *Like it or not here we are to help what can we do?*" That's family. *They are there in the good times and the bad, whether you ask for help or not.*

Teaching by example:

Over and over again we have had conversations with spouses, family members, friends and co-workers where we have made a comment and they heard something different. They not only heard something different, they shared the story to fifty of their closest friends and by the time the story gets back to you, you don't even recognize it. And what is even worse, by the time the story gets back to you your feelings are hurt.

I have found I stick my foot in my mouth much less if I try to talk about subjects I wouldn't mind publishing in the local newspaper. What has always amazed me is that so many people think it is ok to say the first thought that pops into their mind without thinking about who may get hurt by what they say, whether they are saying it in person, email, mail, or phone. Once it is out there, you can't take it back.

I remember as a kid I once told my mother, "Why don't you just slap me? At least the sting of a slap goes away?"

I sometimes go on Facebook so I can see what my son and grandkids are doing and I am sometimes surprised by the things I read. Some of the things my son posts on Facebook surprises me to the point my jaw drops. I have told him that whatever you say in writing follows you FOREVER, but what does a mother know. After all his boss hasn't heard of Facebook, nor anyone else that he might want to build a relationship with in the future. They say the older he gets, the smarter his parents will become. He's 49 and that hasn't happened yet. I hope it happens in my lifetime.

Lesson #14
Every Parent should remember that one day their child will follow their example instead of their advice............by Judie Dietzler

Lesson #15
"Kid's don't care how many sermons you preach to them. The only sermon they'll hear is How you live your life in front of them."........ Bruce Van Horn

Parenting by Example:

Being a good example is behaving in a positive manner. Leading your life in a good way creates a scenario that others will most likely want to copy. For example, when parents demonstrate leadership, strength, guidance and responsibility, their children will absorb the good behavior.

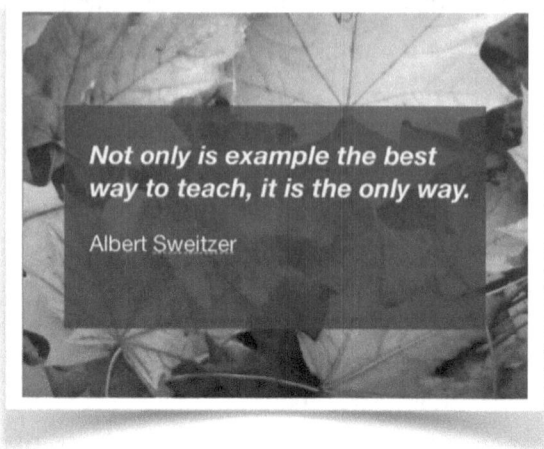

> Not only is example the best way to teach, it is the only way.
>
> Albert Sweitzer

You can't make me be nice. You can't make me be good. You can't make me believe. **But your example, your kindness and behaving in a positive manner is teaching by example.** Leading your life in a good way creates a scenario that others will most likely want to copy. For example, when parents demonstrate leadership, strength, guidance and responsibility, their children will absorb the good behavior.

- "You can't make me be nice. You can't make me be good. You can't make me believe. But your example, your kindness, your patience and love will affect me perhaps enough that eventually I may choose to do those things."

- If your actions were to boomerang back on you instantly, would you still act the same? Doing to others an act you'd rather not have done to you reveals a powerful internal conflict."—Alexandra Katehakis

- "Nothing is so contagious as example; and we never do any great good or evil which does not produce its like."—Francois de La Rochefoucauld

- Children have never been very good at listening to their elders, but they have never failed to imitate them."—James Baldwin

- If our words are not consistent with our actions, they will never be heard above the thunder of our deeds."—H. Burke Peterson

Gossip Destroys Relationships: *People that are setting good examples also have the ability to stop gossip with ease.* Gossip is something that can forever change a friendship, and even prevent you from making new friends in the future. If you're the one gossiping, other people who don't know you will shy away from being your friend. If you talk behind one friend's back, the perception is that you will do that to anyone. ***Don't let the poor behavior of someone else ruin your reputation as a good friend.***

Five Toxic Behaviors That Destroy Family Relationships:

Keeping a family together requires persistent determination to solve every problem and get rid of destructive behaviors.

1. *Insults and Criticism*

2. *Lack of Honesty*
   Deceptive behaviors and lies are destructive, not only for family relationship but also among friends and professionals. Honesty has always been the best most effective long-lasting foundation of any relationship. Lying to avoid responsibility is just another version of deception.

3. *Gossip*
   Gossiping, divulging, spreading lies, and making false accusations about someone in the family are toxic stuffs that destroy family relationships from the inside. When you are gossiping, you indirectly encourage family members to separate and take sides. As a result, there is unnecessary and unhealthy competition between family members, leading to physical and psychological separation.

4. *No Acceptance of Individual Differences*
   Just because someone is family, it does not mean the person has to have the same perspectives towards everything as you do

5. *Failure to Apologize and Forgive*

A Lesson On Anger

When I was a sales trainer, I was so serious about everything. Maybe because so much responsibility was resting on my shoulders. I was the sole bread winner for the family so it was sink or swim. I was building a team in un-chartered territory where people had not heard of Mary Kay Cosmetics and I didn't have time to wait for things to happen, I had to make things happen. I couldn't let my hair down and relax around my beauty consultants because there was always a business image to project.

I remember having conversations with my husband at the time about not discussing any negative comments about any of my consultants with any of their husbands, that was completely off limits. Women and sometimes men can say things that can hurt people's feelings so I had a policy that you never talked about other consultants (unless it was positive) to other consultants, that included husbands. I couldn't afford the negativity among my team. That will destroy a business and friendships quicker than anything else.

In our business there was no room for negativity or petty comments or petty people. I didn't have time or patience for it years ago, and I still don't have the patience for it. Life is too short to sweat over the small stuff.

Ask yourself...Is this going to bother you in five years? If the answer is No! Then why let it bother you now?

I'll give you an example of anger getting out of hand:
One of my Directors called one time and she was furious at another Director. She thought she had done something that she shouldn't have done. She shouted, ranted and raved for approximately forty-five minutes.

I didn't interrupt her once, only making brief comments so she knew I was paying attention.

My husband was in the chair across the room listening and shaking his head. After she finally finished and took a breath she said pointedly, "Well, what are you going to do about it?"

Now I should say that Juanita was no slouch. She had money and she had her own business for years and she was used to getting her own way. But I had one advantage that she didn't have. I had a little better understanding of human nature.

So, I quietly and calmly said "Juanita, I hear what you are saying but to make sure I understand the situation completely could you restate the problem a little slower? I don't know if you're ever been angry before but if I am angry, I can give you everything I've got once but if you ask me to get angry over the same subject a second time it loses the explosive strength, it is more of a dud.

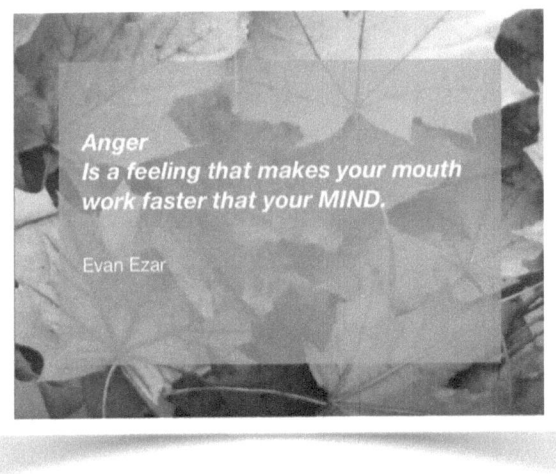

By the time she repeated it she was talking in a normal tone and we were having a conversation. After she finished explaining the problem, I paused to let her think for a minute then I said quietly....

Juanita, I have known Ann for a very long time and I have never known her to do anything similar to what you are describing, not to say it couldn't happen. If it did, I would think that it was probably by accident and if it was me, I would probably give her the benefit of the doubt but this is your situation so let me ask you a question, Juanita. If you were in my shoes and one of your Directors came to you with this problem what do you think would be the best way to handle it? Silence, for what seemed like an eternity, a couple of minutes, then, Juanita said "Well, I think I would probably give her the benefit of the doubt this time, but I'll be watching.

Juanita, I think you made a wise decision. That is exactly the decision I would have made. I am fortunate that you are part of our team and my Director Queen of Sales.

After I hung up my husband asked me "Why do you take that abuse from her?" My response was "I get paid very well to listen to any problems and challenges within my team and I would always prefer they go up with their problems than down. I am equipped to be the complaint department if there is a problem. If a new consultant hears something negative it may be the straw that breaks the camel's back and they will quit before they have a chance to BECOME A STAR."

Women can work in harmony. You just need ground rules. The requirement is a positive attitude and no gossip. If they had a problem, they could always bring it to me but I also asked them to bring at least one potential solution.

I used to do a program in Mary Kay with these little tombstones and a little graveyard and I would say "Here lies _____Born 1945 died................... 1995.......Buried..............2030 That means that between the years 1995 and 2030 she literally existed without playing the "symphony within her."

God gives each of us talents to use for him and to help others. We have only a certain number of days and hours here on earth and we need to make them count for good and to benefit others so that when we are gone, we have left behind a legacy of compassion that will be remembered.

I remember when I first started in Mary Kay Cosmetics, I didn't think I could do it but my Director kept telling me how great I was and she said it so often that I began to believe it. I remembered that lesson and when I moved to Idaho, I always remembered the lesson from my Director and I always told my consultants and Directors how special and great they were.

"Whatever your mind believes will be achieved, and I wanted them to know they could achieve greatness."

"Carry out random acts of kindness, with no expectation of reward, safe in the knowledge that one day, someone might do the same for you." ......Judie Dietzler

There is a wonderful couple in my church, Jan and George, that I have watched help so many people with their loving kindness and helping hand.

CHAPTER 11

LEGACY OF A PARENT

Lesson #35
The way We Treat Our Parents Mirrors Our Future!

Ron's mother died in 2002 and she was one of the nicest ladies I-have met. I am sure she was very opinionated when she was younger. I can relate to her because I feel she had to be strong to survive as a parent, spouse and partial bread winner.

She was only sixty-four when her husband died so she had to learn how to survive and take care of herself almost thirty more years in a day and age when you didn't make much money or receive a pension and only a small social security check.

She was feisty and so was I but she was Ron's mother and I always respected her and always was eager to talk to her and Ron's cousin. She would call and talk to Ron briefly and ask if she could talk to me. I was never disrespectful to her.

Her daughter had gone to a psychologist a few years earlier because she was angry at her mother and dad (he had passed away years earlier). She said the Psychologist told her she should divorce her mother.

I find that hard to believe that any reputable Psychologist would make that suggestion but that was her words. It literally crushed Betty. She was devastated because she adored her daughter.

She had told me about all of the things that she had done with Marlene over the years and how close they had been.

Since I had never had a relationship with my own mother, I couldn't help but think how lucky Marlene was to have had a special relationship and I couldn't understand how she could hurt her mother so deeply.

She not only had that anger inside her but she had passed along the same resentment she feels to her children and grandchildren and robbed them the opportunity to get to know one of the kindest women of the past generation. Betty's daughter didn't even go to her memorial service. I can't comprehend how someone could even think that is acceptable behavior.

I loved spending time with my mother-in-law. We were very different but I liked talking to her because I was able to see a different perspective on whatever topics we were discussing. We were from different generations so we sometimes looked at things differently but we respected each other even when our views were opposing.

I wish the younger generation understood that you can look at a subject differently and still respect the other person. Both sons and their wives seem to look at life so different than my generation did in the past and now and they don't seem to be willing to compromise or look at the world from other people's point of view.

Lesson #36
Always Respect your elders....

To give you a couple of examples: We bought a house last year and while they were still building it one son and his wife were walking through the house with us. Paul said "Did you even look at the plans before they started building the house?" I looked around for his dad who was nowhere in sight.

I would have loved to go into hiding myself but I decided to confront the question head- on. "Yes, I looked at the plans, I even told the builder exactly what I wanted. I designed it this way on purpose. And in case you are interested I don't have dementia so I am pretty good at making decisions."

We went a little farther and his wife pipes up and says "I don't think the bedroom door is wide enough. You won't be able to get your walker through it. At this point I said "Well isn't it fortunate that I don't need a walker but in case I do need one it is handicap accessible."

When we were finished with the walk through, I discovered my husband hiding out in the garage. I asked him why he was in the garage and he said he could tell the way the conversation was heading and he decided to go into hiding. He thought I was better equipped to handle the situation.

Paul and his wife live approximately four-six blocks from our new house but they haven't been back since that day over a year ago but my son and his wife haven't been to our new house either and it's been a year and a half.

I have a couple of friends that live in my community who talk about how their sons are not always the most reliable when it comes to helping when they need a hand with something but they tell me their daughter-in-law's are wonderful. They constantly call and check to see how things are going and if they need any extra help.

They don't want their husband's Mom to get in any dangerous situation of any kind. They say it is so much better to be safe than sorry and they would rather get a call requesting assistance that a call saying they have been taken to the emergency room. Their Motto is "It is better to be safe than sorry."

They realize that if they don't oversea and make sure their parents are in a safe environment now, it could get very costly later on if they should need to look for permanent daily care for their parents or move them in to their home which is not something that their parents would probably want.

Seniors want to be independent and live in their own home for as long as possible. Most of them have not had to rely on someone else since they were at least eighteen years of age and do not want to regress at the age of seventy, eighty or ninety to depend on someone who they used to change their diapers.

Lesson #37
When tempted to criticize your parents, spouse, or children, bite your tongue.

CHAPTER 12

CELEBRITIES FROM THE PAST

A blast from the past:

I was dating a mountain man who lived in Riggins, Idaho a number of years ago when a tall, dark and handsome stranger walked up to the car of my current date & proceeded to flirt with me & ask me on a date. I thought that was extremely bold but I couldn't help but be intrigued. As fate would have it, I didn't date the mountain man for long because he did jet boat tours & my idea of camping is an exclusive resort not a tent.

Bill and I started dating and he liked to do everything first class which fit my style just fine. We would go to Aspen, Las Vegas, etc.

He knew movie stars so we would get to sit at their table when we were at some of the Las Vegas Shows. You will see a couple of pictures of movies stars we hung out with on the next page.

Bill was a great cook & he would fix crab legs but he would always take mine apart for me because it appeared to require an engineering degree to get the crab out of the leg.

Bill was in sales most of the time I knew him. When I met him, he was selling time shares at the Salmon River Resort.

There is a potential downfall of having two people that are in sales dating each other. When you are in sales you are trained to ask a lot of questions as part of the close when you are talking to the client.

Bill and I would go out on a date and I would ask questions as part of our conversation. He would say "Stop closing me." and I would say "I am not closing; this is called a conversation." That is how most of our dates usually went. But he was fun.

Bill was at my house the night before I got married, helping me get ready for the big day & at the same time trying to get me to not marry Ron and to marry him instead. But Ron was such a special guy and I knew he would take good care of me, and I was right. I had spent so many years on such highs and lows that I needed stability in my life and I am so glad God was directing that decision. Since the medical road ahead was going to be so rocky, I not only needed someone that would love me unconditionally but having the stability of medical insurance was going to be important for my survival. Thank you, God, for leading me in the right direction.

Maxine, (one of my friends, Dom Deluise and me

Wayne Newton and me

CHAPTER 13

LIFE'S CRAZIEST MOMENT

Have you ever had a time when you did something that you wish you could have taken it back or started over?

Well so have I.

So, I have combined a few of them in this chapter for your reading pleasure.

Maybe my crazy moments will jog a few of your crazy moments......

Hope you enjoy the offbeat, downright weird, crazy stuff.

Life's Embarrassing Moments

My husband and I were out to lunch today and he decided to go to the restroom. He was gone so long that I thought he fell in but he finally came back and sat down.

That was when he explained his dilemma. He was pulling up his fly (zipper), when half way up it wouldn't move up.

He moved it down even though it didn't really want to go back down. Then tried again to pull it up and at the half way mark it once again stopped and refused to move.

In frustration he tried a couple more times and finally on the forth try the zipper reluctantly gave in ran to the top. Ron gingerly looked to see if the zipper was separating but he sighed with relief when he found the teeth together.

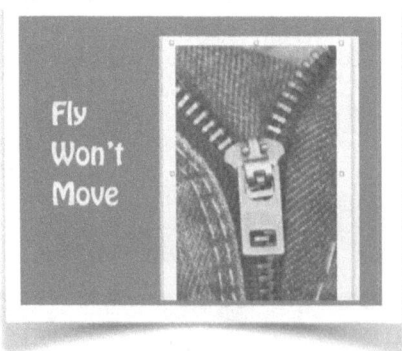

As he sat down and explained his story and I was rolling on the floor laughing with everyone staring at me. Ron then reminds me that his story isn't nearly as embarrassing as the one with me at the Radio Station.

I said "You're right I should probably put it in the book," so here goes.

I was the public relations chair for Soroptimist International of Boise and I had an appointment with one of the executives at one of the radio stations to promote our service projects on air. The office of the executive that I had the appointment with was at the end of a very long hall.

When I arrived the front office secretary called him and he told her to bring me on back to his office.

As we were going down the hall, I noticed that all of the executives in all of the offices along the way were coming out of their offices and greeting me. I couldn't help but notice the friendly atmosphere and enthusiastic reception I received.

After we were finished with our business and had made arrangements for promoting our service projects, the manager of the station walked me up to the front of the building. Once again all of the executives came out of their offices and greeted me and said good bye with a hearty come back and see us again soon.

As I was about to walk out the front door the receptionist came up to me and whispered in my ear," I'm not sure if I should say anything but your skirt is stuck in your pantyhose."

Now speaking of one embarrassing moment, it would have been nice to know that little bit of information before I walked down the long hall to the station managers office.

Another moment..........Thank goodness, not mine.

One of my friends was at a party and another friend walked up to her and said I like your necklace Norva.

Norva, said "I do too, I don't remember where I got it but I really like it." Another friend overheard the conversation and walked up to both ladies and said "I remember where you got it because I gave it to you and it is a book marker." Everyone laughed and Norva said "Well I don't read and it works great as a necklace."

Imagine marking your place in your book with your book mark or if you want to find a new and clever way to use it, wear it around your neck.

Norva has probably figured out a way to attach her book marker to her new wings in heaven

The MK Recruiting Nightmare!

Over the years some wonderful women joined the ranks of Mary Kay as beauty consultants but I did look for people that I felt could project the image. We wore business attire to all of our sales meetings, trainings and seminars.

We taught the Mary Kay's "Golden Rule" philosophy and that Mary Kay believed in God first, family second, and career third.

One day I was at a networking event and a gentleman walked up to me and said he thought his daughter would be perfect for Mary Kay. He said she lived in Nampa, Idaho and asked if I would talk to her. I said I would be happy to sit down with her.

We set a day and time and I met him along with my husband so we could follow him over to her house. When we arrived, I noticed there were dozens of small kittens running around outside the house but I like cats so I didn't think anything else about it until we got inside.

The man that wanted me to meet his daughter walked in first, followed by me and then my husband. We were greeted by the prospective consultant and her husband. The first thing he said was "I hope you don't mind snakes; I don't have any other vices like women, drinking, or smoking so my only vice is snakes. I have a Boa Constrictor and a Python."

I stopped abruptly, and my husband ran into me. I would have immediately turned around and ran at lightning speed out the front door if my husband wasn't blocking the door, so I stood frozen in place.

He said "I bet you were wondering why we have so many cats?" I wasn't really! I just thought they liked cats or forgot to spay them.

He continued, "We have the cats so we can feed them to the snakes." At that point I started to see stars but I knew I needed to keep my wits long enough to get out of the zoo.

The snakes were across the room but both cage doors were open and he casually strolled across the room and picked the boa constrictor up and asked if I would like to hold him.

Holding a snake was the last thing on my mind. Escaping was more in tune to what I had in mind. I tried to make a feeble attempt at maybe some other time if I live to see another day, when he said maybe I would enjoy the tarantula behind me.

Now sheer panic is flooding through every fiber of my body as I am trying to decide how I can escape from this looney ward. Just then his wife said why don't we go in the kitchen and I'll fix some coffee. Since that was one room farther away from the snakes and tarantula, I jumped on that opportunity to exit the room so I moved quickly toward the new location.

It usually takes about forty-five minutes to go through a presentation but I must say I broke a Mary Kay record. She put on the coffee and sat down and I was finished with the presentation before the coffee was finished. I stood up and said: "here is my phone number, give me a call if you have any questions. I hate to run but I have another appointment and I am running late. Here is some literature and I will talk to you soon."

I literally flew out the front door, down the steps and was in the car leaving my husband in the kitchen still saying good-by. It was amazing I didn't pass out from fear because I am deathly afraid of snakes and not much happier with tarantulas.

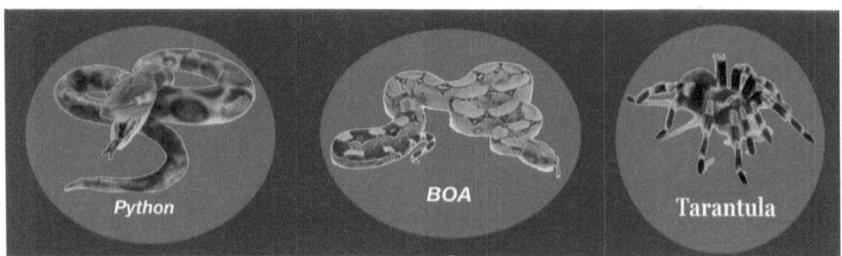

OOPS....We Are Live On Air.....Mrs. Santa Blooper

Channel 7 and Soroptimist Oldster Christmas Program

I happened to be the Public Relations chair for Soroptimist International of Boise and it was time for our Oldsters Christmas Project and Foster Children's Holiday Program. The Idaho Statesman lists Christmas wish items in the paper for local senior citizens and foster children. The community selects people they would like to buy holiday gifts for and what items they would like to purchase.

We have drop off locations throughout the city and we want to make sure the community is aware that the project has started so it is my job to make sure we get the publicity. I contacted KTVB Channel 7 and we were set to go on air with them at 5 am the day after Thanksgiving at one of our Soroptimist members office.

Our members were there, excitement intact including one of my friends dressed as an elf. My husband and I were Mr. And Mrs. Santa. Ten Minutes before we were to go on air our Larry Gebert did a quick on-air promotion but I didn't know we were on air. My Mrs. Santa attire was caught in my underpants so I looked around to see if anyone was watching and it was safe, so I reached behind and adjusted my clothing.

Little did I know that the entire world was watching me grab my butt. So now every year ten of my friends and their husbands have a New Year's Eve party and I have the opportunity to see a replay of Mrs. Santa adjusting her wardrobe on a giant TV screen.

I think I have a section in the book about "How to select your friends" I haven't gone to the party the last couple of years because I started to notice that I am the only one that has blooper events that make it to the big screen. Everyone else must have sedate lives or they just know how to hide the funny stuff.

You can get the full effect of Mrs. Clause's problem with a moving camera. I am making a strange face as if something is hung up and stuck.

The elf runs behind me just as I am trying to nonchalantly figure out what the problem is and fix it without being noticed.

Soroptimist paid no attention and everthing would have been fine with the world but the elf's husband decided to be so efficient and record the event so we could remember it into eternity.

HELLS CANYON ADVENTURE

Ron and I were at a dinner Sunday and a he decided to jump into the middle of a conversation with a few of his stories. He always begins with "I will give you the short version." Then he proceeds with his usual long version.

He decided to tell his "Hells Canyon" story which I had forgotten. I don't know how I could forget it since I was the person that barely lived through it.

I owned a fundraising company and I had a fundraiser scheduled first thing Monday morning in Cambridge, Idaho. That afternoon I had a fundraiser scheduled in Baker City, Oregon.

I asked Ron to give me the quickest and most direct route from Cambridge to Baker City which he did. I drove a large luxurious Cadillac which I jumped in and took off down the road after leaving the Cambridge combination Junior High/High School.

At this point I should mention I have a rather extensive FEAR of heights so you won't find me climbing any Idaho mountains in this century. Idaho has many mountains and a number of them are located in the Cambridge, Idaho area.

I started down the NARROW, TWO LANE MOUNTAIN road heading toward Baker City. About 500 feet down this two-way road (looks like a road for one small vehicle to me) I knew this was a terrible mistake because the road was so narrow only one vehicle could go down or up at a time.

I glanced out the window and noticed there was no guard rail and all I could see was a deep canyon. (At its deepest point Hells Canyon is nearly 8000 feet deep which is deeper that the Grand Canyon) All I could think about was **whatever you do, DON'T LOOK DOWN!**

The road followed the mountain which meant it was not a straight road. It curved constantly. If I could have turned around, I would have. If I could have called a tow truck, I would have but there was no cell service and I wasn't high tech yet so I didn't own a cell phone. My white knuckles clenched the steering wheel during my four-hour ordeal (it takes a while to get to the bottom at 2 miles per hour), with trucks passing me going up the mountain road.

If someone drove up the road I just stopped next to the mountain, closed my eyes and prayed. It was up to the other guy to figure out how to get past me. I sat frozen in place.

I finally reached flat surface and approximately 500 feet away the only sign of civilization was a house so I reluctantly stopped. I have watched way too many unsolved mysteries but fortunately for me the man that answered the door looked fairly harmless.

He gave me directions to Baker City and once again I was on my way. Once I was in town and found a phone. My first call was to Ron who was relaxing at home. (I'm glad someone could relax)

My first question was how much harder would it have been to direct me to a major highway, like I84 so I could have made it to Baker City in an hour instead of four hours and fifteen minutes.

He said it would have taken me an extra fifteen minutes to go back through Weiser and Payette, Idaho before I would get to the freeway.

Let's see how that computes: One hour and fifteen minutes verses four hours and fifteen plus white knuckles, gray hair, and panic.

Yes, I can see how much better the shorter distance worked out.

What happened to your hair?

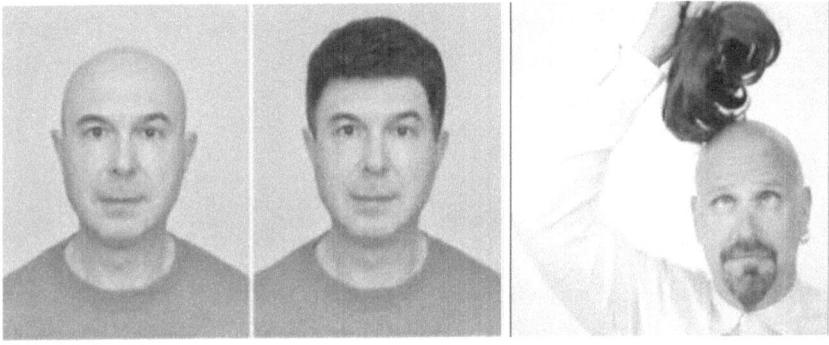

Several years ago, one of my friends, Ken Trefaller, was in the hospital with a mild heart attack. His wife was one of my Mary Kay Directors and they were a great couple. As soon as I heard Ken was in the hospital, we went to the hospital to see how he was doing.

When I walked in, I almost passed out as soon as I saw Ken. He was laying in the bed and looked so quiet and small. He had thick dark brown hair but the man lying in the bed had absolutely NO HAIR.

I turned and ran out of the room, racing down the hall to the nurse's station. I thought I must have got the room numbers confused so I wanted to get the correct room number.

The nurse assured me that I had the right room so I cautiously returned to the room I had just ran from and peered through the door. Just then I heard a voice I recognized say "Hi Judie, it's good to see you, come on in."

I walked through the door not recognizing the face of the person in the bed even though the voice sounded familiar.

He continued, "Don't you recognize me? Oh, maybe you don't recognize me without my darker hair color."

I said no It's not that. I don't recognize you WITHOUT HAIR! I didn't know one of the side effects of a heart attack was that you lose all of your hair.

He started laughing and immediately said. Oh, you didn't know. Obviously, whatever he was talking about I wasn't aware of because I stood there with a blank look on my face.

Ken continued, "I have worn a toupee' for years but when I had the heart attack I thought it was a good time to go natural."

I then got my voice back and said "Well Ken, I could think of a million better times to decide to stop wearing a toupee' than when you just had a heart attack. That was enough to give me a heart attack."

Go Ronnie Go!

I am working an event for one of my businesses and my husband decided to tag along. I had a table at a mall and was demonstrating the Lifetime Vibe and the BioMat. There was an exercise teacher there doing demo's and Ron is not into exercise but he decided he would stand up next to our table and show how great his eighty-one-year-old body was and that he still had a few moves left in him.

I am not sure how impressed she was or how eager she might be to hire him as one of her next instructors and it didn't help attract people to look at the equipment I was demonstrating but it did occupy him for a while.

EVERYDAY MIRACLES

She's probably impressed that he's still got a couple of moves left!

Christmas Present- Afraid of people and his shadow!

We have a seven-year-old Shih Tzu name PePeLePew. We received him from my son and daughter-in law for Christmas seven years ago. He had a very traumatic entrance into our life. Chris and two of my grandkids picked him up one day on the farm where he lived. He was a year old, had never been off the farm and had never been around cars or city noise.

When they got back to my son's house Chris picked him up and accidentally dropped him so for the next two hours five neighborhood women chased him around the neighborhood but he was finally cornered under a car. He was black on the top and white on the bottom but by the time they got him out from under the car he was also black on the bottom because he was covered in oil.

So, Chris decided *"Christmas Present"* needed a bath before they brought him to our house so up to the bathroom they went. After his bath she started to blow dry him and he slithered away, ran under the bed in the master bedroom, was immediately chased out by two cats so he ran down the stairs. Big mistake! In the kitchen he was greeted by two large dogs who immediately chased him back up the stairs. At that moment my son came home and said, "Wonderful, *"Christmas Present"* is here, let's take him out to my mom."

They get to my house and said, "Sit down, close your eyes." As soon as I opened my eyes I looked down and it looked like either a dirty log or a dead skunk. All you could see was two eyes moving back and forth. For the next year every time I wanted to bond with *"Christmas Present"* I had to ask my husband to go get him for me because he would be hiding under the dining table, under my desk or he would be velcro'd to my husband's ankle. Ron would walk PePe over to the grocery store every day and they would sit outside so he could get accustomed to being around people. Customers would walk by and say "What a cute little dog" and reach down and pat him on the head.

Now Ron walks him around our neighborhood and Pepe goes out of his way to find people and other dogs. Everyone loves PePe and he loves everyone. He is very affectionate, always looking for someone to give him attention. I sit at my computer and he sits next to me constantly wanting me to rub his ears or tummy or pat his head. For a long time, I thought he would make a great therapy dog but now I think he just needs therapy. But we love him and so do our neighbors.

Pepe's Escape

We had PePe about a year and he was still skiddish with strangers. I was a presenter at a health fair and I also had a booth at the event. My husband decided to go with me and PePe was going to be home alone. We had a doggy door so he could go out in the back yard anytime and we had a sturdy solid fiberglass fence.

When we got home a few hours later PePe was sitting inside the front door excitedly awaiting our return, however, he looked like the lower half of him was muddy and the floor was muddy which I thought was very strange but I didn't have a chance to digest the information because the phone was ringing.

I answered the phone and it was one of my neighbors. She was excited and said that while we were gone PePe got loose by digging out from under our fence and ran around the neighborhood but no one could catch him. He ran off and now they can't find him.

I said "He couldn't have got out; He's sitting right here looking up at me. He was waiting for us when we walked in the door. It must have been a different dog."

Pat said, "No, it was definitely PePe, go out and check your back yard."

Ron and I went out and checked the gate and sure enough there were two holes. Apparently, PePe wanted to get out and go find Ron because Ron and PePe are joined at the ankle but after running around the neighborhood he must have got scared and decided he better get home before we got home and he couldn't figure out how to crawl through his escape hole so he dug another hole to get back into the back yard and sat there patiently waiting for us to walk through the door.

The only thing that gave him and his little adventure away was the fact that he was very muddy and needed a bath. We couldn't get mad at him because we were so happy that he was safe.

Our house is located one block away from a very busy street and so much could have gone wrong but God even looks after pets. **(Everyday Miracles)**

Everyone needs a pet! They are calming and wonderful companionship. All they require is food and love.

CHAPTER 14

LEGACY OF A HERO

What is a Hero? A Hero is just someone who does what is right, no matter how hard it may be.

You don't need to look in a storybook for a hero-so long as you are honest, kind, and do what is right, you only need to look in a mirror.

Inside this chapter you will see a list of everyday Hero's. If you do your best to do the right thing daily and your #1 mentor is God and with his help you are working to make our world a better place then you are also a Hero among us.

Chapters Included:
- Legacy of a War Hero
- Legacy of Helping Hand "Hero's"

Legacy of a Hero

I have been watching the memorial service of Senator John McCain, an American hero, who is leaving behind a legacy of love and service for his family and our country. I am a registered Republican but I have never voted for a party.

I have always voted for the person I felt would do the best job for our country. I voted for Barack Obama but I am sad that John McCain didn't get a chance to be President. I didn't know until I was listening to the service that in 2008 when he was republican nominee for president, he had a far-out idea of asking a democrat to be his running mate. Can you believe that? So, he called Joe Liberman and proposed the idea and Joe responded with:

"You know, John, I'm really honored, but I don't see how you can do it. Even though I won my last election as an independent, I'm still a registered democrat." And John's response was direct and really ennobling. "That's the point, Joe," he said with a certain impatience. "You're a democrat, I'm a republican. We could give our country the bipartisan leadership it needs for a change."

John made a speech when he returned to the Senate last summer after his surgery. The speech is worth reading but I am going to mention one small excerpt from the speech especially worth" repeating:

"What greater cause could we hope to serve than helping keep America the strong, aspiring, inspirational beacon of liberty and dignity and defender of the dignity of all human beings."

That in short was the McCain American policy. <u>moral, engaged, and strong.</u>

I believe that the first requirement to be President of the United States of America is that you need to be a strong moral, honest leader for the world to see. I want to sit down at my TV or computer with my five grandchildren and have them watch the speeches of our president and aspire to be like the person that is residing in the white house.

The name John McCain is based on the actions of the man John McCain had become. He was a source of hope and inspiration for oppressed people throughout the world, and a source of security for allied countries that share our values.

None of us know how many years, hours, months, weeks, or days we have been allowed here on earth but what I do know is that God gave us the gift of life, and my question is how are we going to make the most of it?

Are we going to waste away our time each day or are we going to make our days and hours count?

I would like to share to story of one of my consultants when I was a sales trainer. She was a beautiful twenty-six years old mother of two who was an aerobics teacher and a beauty consultant part-time who found out she had a tumor in her leg.

They finally had to amputate her leg which was devastating for her and after that point she simply withered away in her bedroom. She didn't want to see visitors or her family, including her small boys. The cancer spread to other parts of her body and she eventually died without coming to terms with the illness nor allowing her family to get close to her. She died alone and miserable without the comfort of her family and her small boys last memory of their mother was a closed door and sadness.

John McCain also had cancer, one of the most aggressive forms, but did he sit around and feel sorry for himself? No Way! His concern was the legacy he would leave behind and the legacy our country is leaving behind. Even with cancer he wasn't thinking of himself.......He was thinking of us.

John McCain made his time count for something. He was a sailor, aviator, husband, warrior, prisoner, hero, congressman, senator, nominee for President of the United States. His life could have been defined from his time as a prisoner of war but it wasn't. That was only a small portion of the overall picture of his life. It helped prepare him for his future but it didn't define his future.

He would have been a President that I would have been proud if my grandkids decided to follow in his footsteps because he didn't allow politics to override his moral judgement. I am unable to say that about every person that is sent to Washington DC because not all have honesty, truth and God on their side. ***In many cases politics is more important to our representatives*** **than doing what's right.**

I would like to share a story that I used many times when I was a sales trainer about how time seems to fly:

Here lies_____(fill in name) born 1945 died 1970 buried 2040 She could have had a full and rich life of helping and serving others but she gave up on life and from 1970 until the end of her life.

Each day was the same as the one before. What she didn't realize is she didn't need to be President in order to make a difference in the world and leave a legacy. You can leave a legacy by helping one person at a time. A little kindness and community service can make a huge difference.

What legacy are you planning to leave behind? *Will it be a Legacy of Love and Compassion that will live on for generations?*

There are so many ways to make a difference in the world: I am going to name 12 but you can do a google search and find so many more:

1. **Join or launch a gift economy:** Gift economies enable people to exchange goods, services and favors without any need for cash payment. One of the best initiatives is free cycle, a global online gifting website based on the idea that one man's junk is another man's treasure.

2. *Start your own alternative currency.* Moving your account from a corporate bank to a credit union is one simple way of active protest too if you can only do one thing, do this!

3. Politicians not listening? *Be the change you want to see! Organize a monthly clean-up operation with like-minded people?*

4. *Say no to GMO with your own community garden.* The best way of protesting GMO foods, boycotting supermarkets and inspiring others to do the same is to get your hands dirty! Gardening is easier than you might think, not to mention rewarding and therapeutic.

5. *Start your own Avaaz campaign.* Avaaz's successes cannot be understated; collectively its members have campaigned for 50 million actions, staged almost 10,000 marches and flash-mobs, raised over $15m for good causes, and taken on politicians and corporations at the highest echelons to win incredible victories on urgent environmental and human rights issues. Now, you can create your own community petition.

6. *Make the most of your unique talents.* We are all good at something, and our special skills can always be used for the good of all. What's your special skill? Have you ever considered using it (free of charge!) to make a positive difference? Maybe you are good with technology and could design a website for a charity or initiative close to your heart. Maybe you are a people person who could fundraise and organize events with a big impact. Maybe you

are creative and could run art workshops for vulnerable people or kids in your community or just volunteer.

7. ***Fund- or create- something awesome.*** Crowdfunding is one of the best things to have happened as a result of the internet. With a click of the mouse you can either create or fund a potentially world-changing project- check out global giving for some ideas of how you can help, or ask for funding to create a project close to your heart.

8. ***Make a statement with guerrilla art.*** Guerrilla art is street art which is exciting, subversive, anonymous and inspiring. Banksy is one of the most celebrate guerrilla artists, making bold political statements through what was once considered graffiti vandalism (his murals are now collectables and sell for big money at auctions, which although sad is a sign of the movement's respect)

9. ***Be kind.*** It may sound obvious, but in our stressful and fast-paced lives it's easy to forget how important small acts of kindness really are. Being nice costs nothing and is probably the most important thing of all we can do, every single day. Treating other people as you would like to be treated will make you feel warm and fuzzy, even if it's just smiling at a stranger on the train or offering your seat to someone who needs it. Pay it forward fantastic initiative (and inspirational book/film) which is based on the idea that for every good deed you receive from another, you pass it on to someone else. Making other people happy is scientifically proven to make you happy too, and what do happy people make? A happy world.

10. ***Websites you can go to volunteer to make a difference in the world:*** http://voicesofsept11.org http://www.projectnightnight.org https://twilightwish.org. https://www.shoesthatfit.org Provides information, support services and events for families, rescue workers and survivors. Grants wishes to senior citizens. Volunteer, donate items, money or your time. Help international human rights

organizations that work to end child trafficking and exploitation. Help provide new shoes to kids in need. Donate packages to homeless children. Help provide for children that include totes include new blanket, children's book & a stuffed animal.

11. ***Write notes of gratitude:*** to the people in your everyday life who make a difference the mailman, a grocery clerk, or the greeter at the mall. Just by paying attention to those who can easily go unnoticed

12. ***Don't forget Common Courtesy and Small Acts Of Kindness.*** Everything you do each & every day positive or negative builds your Legacy.

Never doubt that a small, committed group of citizens can change the world; indeed, it's the only thing that ever has.

Read More: http://www.trueactivist.com/10-ways-to-make-positive-change-in-the-world/

Helping Hand Hero's

A Hero=a person who, in the opinion of others, has special achievements, abilities, or personal qualities and is regarded as a role model or ideal:

There are many people that I feel would qualify as hero's worldwide, that are quietly helping people.

Many of them are in my church and are people we meet every day. Unfortunately, I feel that we lost one of the best humanitarians when we lost John McCain. I did not always agree with his politics but I knew he was honest and trustworthy and that is something very hard to find in Washington DC these days.

If you want to find Hero's you will need to look elsewhere to find them. You don't need to agree with them but you need to trust their heart. If you don't trust their heart you need to look somewhere else for your inspiration and your hero.

Here are fourteen hero's that have been an inspiration:

I am sure you can think of a few of your own:

1. ***Jesus Christ*** was a spiritual Teacher, who preached a gospel of faith, love and forgiveness.

2. ***Princess Diana*** who ended up becoming the "People's Princess because she wasn't afraid to touch people heart to heart. She knew instinctively how to give from her heart.

3. ***Mother Teresa*** was a Roman Catholic nun who devoted her life to serving the poor and destitute around the world. She also founded missionaries for charity, a religious congregation devoted to helping those in great need.

4. ***Martin Luther King*** was one of America's most influential civil rights activists.

5. ***Dalai Lama,*** Spiritual and political leader of Tibetans, a religion based on KINDNESS. We should a jump on that band wagon.

6. ***Nelson Mandela*** considered the father of a democratic South Africa and awarded the Nobel Peace Prize in 1993 for helping to end racial segregation.

7. ***Marie Curie,*** Polish scientist who won a Nobel prize in both Chemistry and Physics and broke down man barriers for women in science.

8. ***Harriet Tubman*** escaped from slavery but returned on many dangerous missions to Maryland where she helped lead slaves to freedom.

9. ***Florence Nightingale***, volunteered to nurse soldiers during the Korean War and she helped improve the standard and prestige of the nursing profession.

10. ***Buddha*** was a young prince who gave up the comforts of palace life to seek the meaning of life by meditating in the wilderness. After gaining realization, the Buddha spent the remainder of his life traveling around India teaching a middle path of meditation and inner peace.

11. ***Eleanor Roosevelt,*** helped draft the United Nations declaration of human rights and strived to improve civil rights in the US. She inspired many people because of her positivity, compassion and self-giving.

12. ***St Therese de Lisieux*** A Carmelite nun, who died at 24, unknown to the world. Yet after her death, her simple writings had a profound effect, becoming one of the best-selling spiritual writings. Her approach was a simple approach of doing the smallest acts with love.

13. ***Eva Peron*** served as Argentina's First lady who inspired millions with her campaigns to help the poor and give women the right to vote.

14. ***Anne Frank,*** was an ordinary teenage girl who wrote an extraordinary diary of her experiences and thoughts on the Holocaust & after she perished her father found the diary and published her story. Even in her writing she retained an optimistic spirit and faith.

Out of the 14 people that used their gifts to help others 9 were women! Never underestimate to contributions that women are making and the legacy they leave behind.

Lesson #38
The greatest gift you can give to God is to take that life and use it to help others.

CHAPTER 15

LEGACY MILESTONES

Life Lessons, the necessary building blocks for life, taught by experience and experts alike!

Throughout my life I have learned many lessons, most of them the road of "Hard Knocks."

I would have loved to have learned these lessons in my twenties instead of spreading it out over a half century.

I sprinkled the lessons throughout the pages of the book but I am listing all of the lessons in one chapter so you will have them as a reference.

So much of life is wasted on worry, regret, pain, and heartache. But I spent too many of my younger days on needless worry. I simply didn't know better.

I suppose "life lessons" are called that for a reason. You need to experience life in order to learn the lessons. And the more life you experience, the more lessons you accumulate.

However, some extremely valuable lessons I learned from other people. Some I discovered from reading great thinkers like Oprah, Deepak Chopra, and Mary Kay Ash.

Although some lessons must be learned through experience, you don't have to wait until you're old to become aware of what's truly meaningful and worthwhile. You simply need the curiosity and desire for self-awareness and personal growth.

Once you learn the lessons, you can apply them in your life at any age and see the benefits to your happiness and well- being.

My Life Lessons
(From the last half century)

Lesson #01
"Spend Less Time Deciding Who's Right, And More Time Deciding What's Right!"....Unknown

Lesson # 02
"Pick & Choose Your Battles Wisely".....quote by Craig T Owens

Lesson #03
"Don't Make Every Situation A Battleground" ...quote by Judie Dietzler

Lesson #04
"Only you give your past Power" .....Oprah

Lesson #05
"Do Everything With Integrity, Honesty & Principle".....quote by Judie Dietzler

Lesson #06
"Your attitude determines your altitude. If you think you can, you can; and if you think you can't you're right" ......quote by Mary Kay Ash

Lesson #07
"Aerodynamically, the bumble bee cannot fly, but the bumble bee doesn't know it so it goes on flying anyway"......quote by Mary Kay Ash

Lesson #08
"Don't limit yourself. Many people limit themselves to what they think they can do. You can go as far as your mind lets you. What you believe, remember, you can achieve"... quote by Mary Kay Ash

Lesson #09
"Fear is faith that it won't work, Everyone has obstacles to overcome, but those with the great faith can conquer whatever stands in the way"..... quote by Mary Kay Ash

Lesson #10
"Courage is being Scared but saddling up anyway".... quote by John Wayne

Lesson #11
"You can't stand still. You either go forward or backward. Failures are not failures, they are learning experiences that will help us grow & succeed in life if we take the time to learn from them"......quote by Judie Dietzler

Lesson #12
"Don't let the negatives of life control you. Rise above them. Use them as your stepping stones to go higher than you ever dreamed possible" ...... quote by Mary Kay Ash

Lesson #13
"If it's Meant To Be It's Up To Me" ....quote by Robert H Schuller

Lesson #14
"Actions Speak Louder Than Words" ..... quote by Abraham Lincoln

Lesson #15
"How You Treat Your Parents Is How Your Children Will Treat You" .....quote by Judie Dietzler

Lesson #16
"Every Parent should remember that one day your child will follow your example instead of your advice" .... quote by Judie Dietzler

Lesson #17
"When you reach an obstacle, turn it into an opportunity. You have the choice. Refuse to throw in the towel. It is far better to be exhausted from success than to be rested from failure" ...... quote by Mary Kay Ash

Lesson #18
"God Does The Thinking But We Need To Do The Leg Work" .....quote by Judie Dietzler

Lesson #19
"Real Beauty begins on the inside and shines through to the outside"... quote by Judie Dietzler

Lesson #20
"Don't worry that you can't give your kids the best of everything. Give them your very best" ......quote by Jackson Brown Jr.

Lesson #21
"It's not what happens to you in life that's important, it's how you interpret what happens to you" .....quote by Judie Dietzler

Lesson #22
Serving creates a meaningful Legacy. ......Author unknown If you want meaning in your life, start with serving others. Find a way to make a difference, even a small difference, and your life will feel purposeful.

Lesson #23
"A successful marriage depends on two things: Finding the right person & being the right person"...... quote by Robert A. Rohm Ph.D.

Lesson #24
"Live so that when your children think of fairness, caring, & integrity, they think of you"...... quote by H Jackson Brown

Lesson # 25
Sometimes we don't realize "When something major happens in our life it should be a wakeup call that we have been given the opportunity to "make changes in our life and the life of others in a huge way and we shouldn't throw that gift away." ....quote by judie Dietzler

Lesson #26
"The dream of personal accomplishment is not nearly as important as God's purpose for our life." .....quote by judie Dietzler

Whether you are my family or your family is in China, Russia, or Washington DC.

Lesson # 27
"The grass is not greener on the other side of the fence. It is just different. The problems you had in this marriage will go with you because the problems are inside you. For things to change, you need to change" .... quote by Judie Dietzler

Lesson #28
"Walking with a friend in the dark is better than walking alone in the light." ......quote by Hellen Keller

Lesson #29
"A friend is a cheerleader when you win, a counselor when you lose, a confidante when you need to share, and a clown when you're feeling blue." …...Unknown (it is rare we can find a female friend that qualifies as the above shining example that you can confide in and she will hold your confidence and never gossip about you. If this is your friend cherish her. She is a rare gem indeed)

Lesson #30
"Friends walk in when everyone else walks out"…. quote by Judie Dietzler

Lesson # 31
"Look For Friends That Bring Out The Best In You"……. Quote by Henry Ford (This is important, If it is a negative relationship or they gossip about you to others, walk away)

Lesson #32
A True friend applauds your strengths, understands your weaknesses, appreciates the combination that is you, & never gossips about you to other people……….Unknown

Lesson #33
"The seeds you plant in the hearts and minds of others will be what you receive in return – Only sow that which you wish to receive in return. Sow good, receive good!" ……. quote by Mary Kay Ash

Lesson #34
"The greatest discovery of all time is that a person can change his future by merely changing his attitude"…..quote by Oprah

Lesson #35
"What's interesting about subscribing to a life of giving is that you become addicted"……quote by Mary Kay Ash

Lesson #36
"Everyone has obstacles to overcome, but those with great faith can conquer whatever stands in the way"…..quote by Mary Kay Ash

Additional Words to Live By………….

Lesson #37
"Think in terms of what's good for the other person" and success in both life and business will seek you out……………. quote by Judie Dietzler

Lesson #38
"Make it a habit of shutting down conversations that tears others down"..........quote by Judie Dietzler

Lesson #39
"We are meant to use and increase whatever God has given us. And when we do, we shall be given more"......quote by Mary Kay Ash

Lesson #40
"The best Legacy you can pass on is by living a Values-Based Life and sharing it with others"......quote by Judie Dietzler

Lesson #41
"Don't compare your life to others and don't judge them. You have no idea what their journey is about".....Author Unknown

Lesson #42
"Make peace with your past so you won't mess up the present".....quote by Marcia Casar Friedman

Lesson #43
"Choose Kindness...and watch it change your life"......quote by Wayne Dyer Kindness & compassion are the principal things that make our lives meaningful. These qualities are our primary source of joy & happiness because they are the qualities from which honesty, forgiveness, patience and generosity flow and are the foundation of a good heart. With a good heart, a good life will follow.

Lesson #44
"Accept conditions as they exist, or Accept responsibility for changing them".....quote by Denis Waitley

Lesson #45
"We choose our joys and our sorrows long before we experience them".....quote by Kahlil Gibran

Lesson #46
"You are always one choice away from changing your life"…..quote by Mac Anderson

Lesson #47
"Don't let someone else's opinion of you become your reality." …..quote by Les Brown

Lesson #48
"Great minds discuss ideas. Average minds discuss events. Small minds discuss people." …..quote by Eleanor Roosevelt,,

Lesson #49
"Do not go where the path may lead, go instead where there is no path and leave a trail." …..quote by Ralph Waldo Emerson,,

Lesson #50
"Greatness is not found in possessions, power, position, or prestige. It is discovered in goodness, humility, service, and character." …..quote by William Arthur Ward

Take these lessons to heart and make them your mantra for living and you will be a success no matter where your journey takes you. It would be my desire that you have a Christian mentor that is at least a season ahead of you in the walk of life.

Whether you have a mentor or not use the lessons in this book as a secondary source along with your two primary sources that will guide you on your lifelong journey:

1. Prayer, God will guide you (be sure and watch for *"Everyday Miracles"*)

2. Your Bible will be your #1 resource book to guide you daily.

CHAPTER 16

LEAVE A WORTHY LEGACY

We all want to leave our mark on this world-to know that our life mattered. What does it mean to leave a legacy? It means putting a stamp on the future, and making a contribution to future generations.

People want to leave a legacy because they want to feel that their life mattered. Once you know what you want your legacy to be, you can start building on it:

Deciding what your legacy will be can help you with all the following:

You can start living in the way you want to be remembered.

It will allow you to start doing what matters, now.

Knowing what you want your legacy to be will allow you to make better use of your time and other resources.

It will influence your day-to-day decisions in a positive way.

Gaining clarity on what you want your legacy to be can give your life meaning and purpose.

It will enable you to allow the legacy that you're building to determine how you show up in the world each day. You will live your life as if you matter. ***Next are ways you'll find to identify the legacy that you want to leave behind after you're no longer here.***

Picture Your 80th Party
Most of us are familiar with Stephen Covey's obituary exercise. Covey indicates that you should imagine your funeral. Then, you should ask yourself questions like the following:

> Who would give a eulogy at your funeral?
> What will they miss about you?
> What positive attributes will they associate you with?
> How are they describing you?

Imagining your funeral is a little macabre, so a variation of this exercise is to picture your 80th birthday party. Everyone you've had an impact on, or have influenced in some way. As they get up to toast you on your birthday, what would you like them to say about you? That's what you want your life to stand for.

What words do you want etched on your tombstone?

Before his death, Thomas Jefferson–the third president of the United States–gave instructions on what he wanted on his grave site. Jefferson wanted an obelisk with the following engraved on it:

Here was buried Thomas Jefferson Author of the Declaration of American Independence of the Statute of Virginia for religious freedom & Father of the University of Virginia.

Most of us won't have anything nearly as grand as Jefferson to put on our tombstones. Nonetheless, an ordinary life lived well and lived with grace can make an important difference in the lives of others. What words do you want etched on your tombstone?

Here are *10 questions to* ask yourself to **identify the legacy you would like to leave.**

- What do you want your life to stand for?
- How do you want to be remembered by your family and friends?
- What will those beyond your circle of family and friends remember you for?
- What kind of an impact do you want to have on your community?
- How will the world be a better place because you were in it?
- What contributions do you want to make to your field?
- Whose lives will you have touched?
- What lessons would you like to pass on to future generations?
- What do you want to leave behind?
- How can you serve?

Brainstorm ways in which you can leave a legacy by using the following ideas as a jumping off point:

1. Add knowledge to your field.

2. Leave a legacy through your body of work.

3. Write a book. (We can literally redirect other people's lives with a word or an action.)

4. Leave money for your descendants that serves as a foundation on which they can build their financial futures.

5. Bequeath money to charities that are near and dear to your heart.

6. Write down family recipes and family traditions.

7. Serve as a good role model. (and look for the good in people)

8. Pass down a heirloom.

9. Be a mentor.

10. Volunteer.

11. Start a business or a non-profit organization.

12. Write your memoir. You can also record video messages for your loved ones, create a scrapbook for them, or create a web site dedicated to your legacy.

13. Write a legacy letter — write down everything you'd want to tell your loved ones if you knew you didn't have long to live. Be sure to capture the essence of who you are by writing about your life lessons, values, accomplishments and hopes. Think of it as an emotional heirloom.

14. Endow a scholarship to your alma mater for future students.

15. Start a blog. (write something worth reading or do something worth writing." …..Benjamin Franklin)

16. Pass down handmade items, such as quilts, cedar hope chests, or wooden crafts.

17. Start a new program in your community, such as starting a recycling program; planting a community garden; or constructing a playground.

18. Pass down skills and know-how.

19. Right a wrong.

20. One of the best ways to live a good story is to focus on what you are passionate about and do that. (Passion brings out passion in others & it will amaze you how as you begin to let your passion shine, others truly will feel liberated to do the same around you.)

21. Live your legacy: Our children listen to us most intently by watching us live. So, live with character, conviction, and passion. The most indelible legacy is the way we live.

22. What are your morals, values, and beliefs? Would I want others to follow in my footsteps?

23. Was I a good friend? How will my friends remember me?

24. Did I live a respectable life that others would use as an example to follow?

"Immortality is to live your life doing good things, and leaving your mark behind." .....quote by Brandon Lee

The legacy we leave is not just in our possessions, but in the quality of our lives. The greatest waste in all of the earth, which cannot be recycled or reclaimed, is our waste of the time that God has given us each day." .....quote by Bill Graham

What will your legacy be?
What will live on after you're gone?
Live your best life by creating a legacy you can be proud of.

CHAPTER 17

LEGACY LIFE LESSONS

Twenty-Three additional Important Life Lessons

Here are life lessons that have stood the test of time:

1. *Live every day as if it was your last.... Give every day your best.*
   We keeping waiting for something amazing to happen that will be the key to our happiness and we forget to experience everything life has to offer. Learn to love right now, and you'll have an amazing life.

2. *Relationships should be our #1 Priority*
   At the end of the day, what matters most are the people in our lives. Put them first every single day. Before work. Before the computer. Before your hobbies. Treat them like they are your everything. Because they are.

3. *Spend below your means*
   Save money. Wait until you can afford it. Live free. Our children learn by your actions, not by what you tell them. Practice what you preach.

4. *Declutter your life*
   The less stuff you have the freer you are. Purchase mindfully, Simplify. Things gather dust!

5. *Create more fun in your life.*
   Don't worry about what other people think of your fun. Just enjoy it. Life is short. You should enjoy it.

6. *Don't be afraid of failure....*
   If you avoid failure, you avoid taking action. Expect and accept that failure is part of the experience. Learn from it, grow from it, and move on.

7. *Friendships need care.*
   One of the top five regrets of the dying is that they let their friendships fade away. Friendships need time and attention. They need to be prioritized not just in word but in deed. Nurture them like a prized garden. The payoff is so worth it. Prioritize experiences. Your positive memories from great experiences far outweigh material things. If you're trying to decide between the new sofa or the family trip, take the trip every time.

8. *Anger is a destructive emotion.*
   The temporary good feeling lasts only briefly, but the repercussions last far longer. Regret, stress, and unhappiness are the byproducts of angry outbursts. Learn healthier ways to communicate your feelings, and when anger arises, step away until it dissipates.

9. *Kindness matters.*
   Small expressions of kindness have an enormous positive impact on other people and on your own happiness. It doesn't take much to be kind. Practice it every day, in every situation, until it's your natural way of being.

10. *Grudges cause pain.*
    Holding on to a grudge is like injecting poison into your body every day. Forgive and let go. There's no other way.

11. *You aren't always right.*
    There's always more than one version. There are many perspectives that are valid. Keep yourself open to that truth.

12. Time Heals.
Whatever is causing you worry or pain right now won't cause you worry and pain forever. Time heals. Things change. It will pass.

13. Define Your Life.
Decide what makes life worth living for you, and then design your life around that.

14. Change is good. Life is change.
We shouldn't resist it. Remaining stagnant is in opposition to the natural order of life. Flow with change. Embrace it and regard it as an adventure.

15. You can't control others.
We can't and shouldn't try to control others. Instead, embrace differences and honor the uniqueness of the people in your life.

16. Gratitude increases happiness.
It is better to focus on what you have rather than thinking about what you don't have. Gratitude fosters positivity and well-being.

17. Serving creates a meaningful legacy.
If you want meaning in your life, start with serving others. Find a way to make a difference, even a small difference, and your life will feel purposeful.

18. Intuition counts.
Your judgment is important, but your intuition supercharges your judgment. Intuition is data from your subconscious mind, based on your past experiences and patterns in life.

19. Don't employ the philosophy "It's my way or the highway."

20. Don't become too attached to outcomes or beliefs.
Open you mind to all possibilities & ideas.

21. The words you speak have power. Consider your words carefully.
Use them for good rather than harm. Once they are out, you can't take them back.

22. Make every day count.
Ask yourself every morning, "What can I do to make today count?"

23. Love, understanding & compassion are the answer to making our world a better place to live.
They are the force for good in this often painful, and harsh world. Share them freely.

I would like to share legacy story that Rev David Hutchinson read one day in his church service May 1, 2005:

A young woman had been diagnosed with a terminal illness. She was given three months to live. And as she was getting her things in order, she called her pastor and asked him to come over. When he got there, she told him what songs she wanted sung at her funeral and showed him the dress she would be buried in.

She described to him her will. She told him how it would care for the family. How her two children would be provided for.

And how instead of giving each of them $100,000 she was giving them each $95,000. $10,000 would be given to the church. She said "really, what difference is there between 100,000 and 95,000 to them. It'll be ALMOST the same. "But THINK" she said "what 10,000 will mean to the church!". "Think" she said. And he thought. Boy did he think.

And she was right - it did make an impact. But that's another story.

Then she said, "OH, I almost forgot!" "There's ONE more thing". "It's very important" "What is it?", her pastor asked. "I want to be buried with a FORK in my right hand". "A fork I don't understand?"

She explained, "My grandmother once told me that at church potluck dinners I should always remember ONE thing. "Keep your FORK". "It was my FAVORITE part "my grandmother said to me. It was her favorite part because she KNEW something BETTER was coming. Something like apple pie chocolate cake. Something wonderful.

SO, when people see the FORK in my hand at my funeral, I want YOU to say, "Keep your fork the BEST is YET to come." "The BEST is yet to come." Right there, in this playful way, she was telling her pastor more about heaven than he ever knew. It was the last time he would see her on THIS earth. But people could not stop - talking about her faith.

Her legacy was to proclaim to the world: *"The BEST is yet to come."*

So just remember……God's gift to you was your life. If you take your life and use your talents and gifts to benefit God and Humanity………….,,
THEN YOU CAN COUNT ON THE BEST IS YET TO COME!

Keep Your Fork………………
The Best Is Yet To Come!

CHAPTER 18

WILL YOUR LEGACY "DASH" LIVE ON?

I want my final chapter of my book to end with the story of "The Dash" by Linda Ellis and Mac Anderson.

If you don't have a copy of the book and DVD, I suggest you get a copy. It is so powerful that I want it to be played at my eventual memorial service because it has such a powerful meaning.

The words of "The Dash" will go straight to your heart.

This story is the best way I know how to illustrate the importance of making the most of the time we have been given here on earth.

I have a dear friend that recently lost her husband much too soon and I nearly lost my husband in 2016. I am sure she envisioned growing old with her husband much the same as I picture with my husband until the ripe old age of 100 but sometimes it doesn't always work out the way we plan.

What I know for sure is that whatever time I have been given I want to make sure I leave behind a legacy that is worthy of the time God granted me here on earth.

My greatest desire is that "My Dash" Will Make A Difference and touch a life for the better.

"The Dash" represents what my book is about:
I hope this message means as much to you as it did me.

"The Dash" Making A Difference With Your Life!

(as told by Linda Ellis and Mac Anderson in their book and video presentation called "The Dash")

I read of a man who stood to speak at the funeral of a friend.

He referred to the dates on tombstone from the beginning...to the end.

He noted that first came the date of her birth and spoke of the following date with tears, but he said what mattered most of all was the dash between those years.

For that dash represents all the time that she spent alive on earth and now only those who loved her know what that little line is worth.

For it matters not, how much we own, the cars, the house, the cash. What matters is how we live and love and how we spend our dash.

So, think about this long and hard: are there things you'd like to change? For you never know how much time is left that can still be rearranged.

If we could just slow down enough to consider what's true and real, and always try to understand the way other people feel.

And be less quick to anger and show appreciation more and love the people in our lives like we've never loved before.

If we treat each other with respect and more often wear a smile remembering that this special dash might only last a little while,

So, when your eulogy is being read with your life's actions to rehash, would you be proud of the things they say about how you spent your dash?

Living Your Dash:

Your time here on earth is limited. Every moment that goes by a piece of your life is behind you. Your days are numbered and each one that passes are gone forever.

If you knew the length of time you were given to live "YOUR DASH" would you make different decisions today and tomorrow on how you are spending your dash?

Would your dash have more meaning when you open your eyes each day?

Imagine yourself with only thirty days left to live your dash. What decisions would you make? What legacy would you be working to leave behind?

If each of us lived as if we had one month to live, I believe we would spend our days differently. I think we would experience more fulfilling lives and we would not only have an eternal legacy but we would leave behind a worthwhile legacy here on earth.

There are so many things about our lives that we don't have control over including when we are born, who are parents are and when we die but God gave us the control to make our own decisions: We get to decide how we're going to use our dash. How are you spending your dash?

Are you living your dash, knowing fully who you are and why you're here? Or dashing to live, hurriedly spending precious time chasing things that really don't matter to you."

(Psalms 90:12) "Teach us to number our days and recognize how few there are; Help us to spend them as we should."

God wants us to realize that our time on earth is limited so we will spend it wisely. But he gives us the choice about how we spend this most valuable currency.

If you go to a cemetery you will discover that entire lives are reduced to two dates and one little dash. What it really comes down to is "What's in the dash?"

I sometimes look at the dash of an individual person's marker and wonder. Was she surrounded by love at the end? What was her passion? Did she have any regrets? Did she leave behind a worthwhile legacy?

CHAPTER 19

THE MIRACLE OF "EVERYDAY MIRACLES"

How I survived To Write Everyday Miracles!

Originally the thought for my life story began because on many occasions my fifty-year-old son would talk to his wife about his childhood and teen years. The stories he told didn't remotely resemble anything that I remembered from his years living at home so I decided I should write down the facts of the years in question.

While I was at it, I decided to write my life story but that wasn't going to be easy because there were major gaps in my memory. I had many traumatic events that happened during my childhood and teen years. They were so devastating that I have blocked them from my memory for most of my life.

For the last twenty-five years I have been counseling clients that have been victims of trauma and I have told them that their brain will release the information when they are ready to handle it. But because I had unresolved trauma it affected relationship decisions I made throughout my life and I have always had a tendency to not trust men or develop close friends.

As I began writing something happened that I didn't expect. I started having memories from the past and they began flowing onto the pages of the computer screen. Suddenly the memories from the past became part of my current reality and I began putting the shattered pieces together, then the tears started to flow and have kept coming day after day.

I have gone between saying "I'm going to publish this book" to "I have no intention of publishing it. "No one wants to read a book that has pain, heartache, and tears mixed in between the pages."

I have prayed about it and in church recently I believe I got the answer to my prayer. A voice spoke to me and said "This book isn't about me, it's about **Everyday Miracles**, and I should go home and change the book to reflect it. It isn't my book; it is a book about how I survived trauma & hardships and how my prayers were answered and I wasn't alone. God was with me, guiding me each step of the way." I hope I can do it justice. God has been with me throughout my life even when I thought I was alone.

So, I went home, changed the name of the book, restructured it, and made sure you would know at what point in the book the *"Everyday Miracles"* happened. I am an ordinary person, with only the talents God has given me. Once I started writing I immediately knew that God had been walking beside me, even in my darkest hours when I thought I was all alone without a friend in the world. I survived because God was guiding me.

Like all children I wanted and needed love but what I found was neglect and abuse from the people that were supposed to love and protect me. You look to your Mother to always love you but she abandoned me and said she didn't care if I lived or died.

My life went from bad to worse as I floated through relationships and toxic chemical exposure but along the way there were *"Everyday Miracles"* and throughout the book I share a half century of Lessons I have learned. Life would have been simpler if I had been taught these life lessons in my twenties. My life finally turned around in my thirties and you will definitely want to stick around for Chapter 16.

Through it all, I know the importance of leaving a worthwhile 'legacy 'and not just existing. It's not too late to start a "legacy of love, compassion and service." My book will show you how. I have gone from the depths of despair to the pinnacle of success not realizing that I wasn't alone after all. There was someone walking beside me, guiding and protecting me along my painful journey. I couldn't have asked for a better advisor, God. My wish is that as you travel with me you may find hope and your own *"miracles"* to **build a legacy to pass to future generations.**

"Everyday Miracles" is a labor of love even though I have cried a bucket of tears and relived the trauma from my past that had been buried for over fifty years.

Would my life be different if I had made different decisions? Definitely Yes! But sometimes what starts out as disastrous decisions leads us eventually to a place where we are able to help and serve others because of our past experiences.

I believe that if I had not gone down this path, I would not have been able to touch and be part of the many lives and experienced their growth, successes and healing along the way. My first husband was a kind soft spoken man and God knew I deserved a kind soft spoken man so he saw fit to send me another wonderful man when I turned forty. I guess he figured I was old enough to appreciate quality when he showed up on my doorstep, and I definitely did. He was a keeper.

The book almost never had the opportunity to get written for the following reasons:

When we were moving into our house, I had two major falls which caused a traumatic brain injury with memory loss so it was important for me to rely on all of my documents and photos over the years to help put together the pieces of my life. I own an Apple computer and the main reason for this brand is that they never get viruses or hacked. A few months ago, while I was on technical support with Apple, they informed me that my computer was approximately ten years old (like I didn't know that bit of information), and I should probably think about getting a new one.

I wasn't having any problems with my current computer but I decided to get a new IMAC. They transferred everything from one to the other and as it would happen someone walked by and bought my computer while I was in the Apple store.

Four weeks after getting my new computer home I got a virus on my computer and tech support supposedly fixed it. One week later I got a second virus and tech support said we needed to back everything up to the cloud and for the next hour that is what the technical support agent said we were doing. At that point he proceeded to reformat my hard drive. As a precaution I emailed my book and everything on my desktop to myself. Once he was finished, he said my firewall was secure and I should have no more problems.

After I hung up, I wanted to work on my book and discovered I no longer had a book in iBook. I had absolutely no documents or pictures from my entire life. I am a videographer and I had many completed videos in iMovie and they were gone. I didn't even have the iMovie application. I had emailed my book to my email account but it was a .pdf and I couldn't edit it so I had to re-write it.

But there is a real miracle to the story. If I had not started writing the story in July and adding pictures from my life to the book, then emailed it to my personal account before Apple re-formatted my hard drive, **there would be NO BOOK. (*Everyday Miracle*)**

I needed the documents and pictures to help piece together my life. The only pictures of my life that I have left are the pictures in my book. There is no doubt that miracles happen every day and God is guiding the miracles.

I believe God directed me to start to write the book at that precise time because he knew what was going to happen in the near future and he was preparing me in advance. I wasn't able to save everything but the most important pictures were saved. Last week I took my computer into the Apple store to the Genius Bar to a technician named Tyler who happened to be very compassionate. After listening to my story, he worked on my computer and asked his boss for additional time to help me and another ***"Everyday Miracle."***

My four-year-old granddaughter drowned in 1998 and I had a ton of beautiful pictures of her on my computer that had been erased. They were deleted from the cloud but they didn't delete. Tyler was able to retrieve them for me. *Another reason to start believing in Miracles! I hope my miracles will help you find a few miracles in your life. Look for them... Expect them.*

www.ingramcontent.com/pod-product-compliance
Lightning Source LLC
Chambersburg PA
CBHW030107100526
44591CB00009B/319